Conversations
with Animals

Conversations *with* Animals

Cherished Messages and Memories
as Told by an Animal Communicator

LYDIA HIBY
with
Bonnie S. Weintraub

NEWSAGE PRESS

CONVERSATIONS WITH ANIMALS

NewSage Press
PO Box 607
Troutdale, OR 97060-0607
503-695-2211
FAX 503-695-5406

Visit our web site: www.newsagepress.com

Cover Design by George Foster
Book Design by Patricia Keelin and Nancy L. Doerrfeld-Smith

Printed in the United States on reycycled paper with soy ink.

Distributed by Publlishers Group West in the United States
(800-788-3123) and in Canada (416-934-9900)

Cover Photo: When Lydia Hiby was four years old, her father, Carl Hiby, photographed this special moment between Lydia and an animal friend in the park.

Library of Congress Cataloging-in-Publication Data

Hiby, Lydia, 1958-
    Conversations with animals : cherished messages and memories as told by an animal communicator / by Lydia Hiby with Bonnie S. Weintraub.
      p.   cm.
    Includes bibliographical references (p.   )
   ISBN 0-939165-33-3
    1. Human-animal communication.   2. Domestic animals—Behavior.
I. Weintraub, Bonnie S., 1944-   . II. Title.
QI 776.H535   1998
636.089 -dc21
                                 98-7461
                                 CIP

4   5   6   7   8   9   10

DEDICATIONS

In memory of Kodiak who was the inspiration for this book.

d'Kamron Kodiak
November 3, 1990 — July 14, 1999

In loving memory of my mother, Joan Hiby,
who nurtured and encouraged my love for the animals.
For all the animals who have gently taught me
every step of the way and who love us all unconditionally.
And for Kodiak and Bonnie Weintraub
who both graciously decided to walk along my path for a while
in order to give birth and life to this book.
I am truly blessed.

– Lydia Hiby

In memory of my beloved Kodiak,
who touched my life with his grace and dignity.
To all the animals of the world who share
a special relationship with a human.
In loving memory of my mother, Myra Ehrenhaus,
who instilled in me the belief
that every kind of education is valuable,
and for my father, Dr. Jesse Ehrenhaus,
who told me, "Never rest on your past laurels."
And for Crispin,
who has made my heart smile once again.

– Bonnie S. Weintraub

Acknowledgments

I have been very fortunate to have wonderful people and animals, placed by divine guidance, who have helped me in my life, my work, and with this book.

Most important, I want to acknowledge Bonnie Weintraub who became my voice with such accuracy—no one else could have done such an incredible job. Blessings to Bonnie. And to the Weintraub family, Barry, Dani, Jeffrey, and Brandi, who welcomed me into their family while I borrowed their mom for the past year.

For my family foundation, I thank my dad, Carl Hiby, my brother Greg Hiby, and all extended Hiby and Gerhard family. Also, Virginia Hoyt, Richard Gorman, and Inslee Barnett, dear friends and part of my surrogate family. And the members of my animal family, past and present, who have taught, healed, and energized me.

For my training as an animal communicator, Beatrice Lydecker saw my potential, encouraged me, and passed on her knowledge so that I could also help improve the lives of owners and their beloved pets. Henry Randazzo, D.V.M., Steve Liebl, D.V.M., and the staff at Bay Animal Hospital gave me a home away from home, and allowed me to grow without judgment as I started practicing my communication skills. John Ottaviano, O.M.D., John Limehouse, D.V.M., and Robert Anderson, D.V.M., patiently answered all my questions on natural healing of animals and allowed me to spend quality time at their clinics. These opportunities helped me to acquire a well-rounded education of holistic medicine.

My friends, Jackie Sinnott and Marvin Happell, provided for my well-being at a time when I needed them both. And my wonderful circle of women friends whose strength carried me through my weak moments and whose insights gave me better clarity—*thank you* Rainy Lee Kemp, Francis Welker, Gayle Uyehara, Annemarie Finley, Mary Edwards, Jane Difloure, Peg Bergmeyer, Helga Kane, Mary Childs, and Gesa Brinks.

I am grateful to Bill Delano, Randall Hayward, Maryann Harville, and Kat Gayson at Triangle Training Center for my Dolphin Encounter. And to all my wonderful clients and their special companions for sharing a part of their lives, and being receptive to hearing a different perspective and giving me validation, which built my confidence.

Special thanks to Maureen R. Michelson, the publisher at NewSage Press, for her vision to say *yes* to two novices in the book world, and for her careful editing of the manuscript. Also, Cindy McKechnie, who was our first contact at NewSage Press. And to Tracy Smith for her attention to editing details, and for being a fresh voice in the final push to complete the book. Thank you all. The future looks bright.

Lydia Hiby

ACKNOWLEDGMENTS

The chain of events—from Kodiak's accident, to meeting Lydia, and uniting with NewSage Press—was not coincidence. This sequence of happenings was synchronicity at its finest. The people and animals who journeyed with me as I wrote were not placed there by chance. Their energy strengthened the thread I used to weave Lydia's stories into words of truth—bringing her dream to fruition—and ultimately raising human consciousness about animals.

Looking back, the fact that I was a fledgling writer worked in my favor. I ignored the negatives. I never lost sight of our goal or considered stopping short of completion. Instead, I embarked on this venture with a passion and optimism owned by an innocent. And always by my side was Kodiak, whose dark brown eyes seemed to say, Keep going.

To those who have championed me, becoming my rock, my sounding board and replenishing my spirit—I thank you. First and foremost, I am grateful to Lydia Hiby for choosing to take me on this incredible adventure. I am honored to have made her dream come true. I cherish her friendship.

For their special support, I thank my family, in particular my husband, Barry, who watched with amazement that turned into pride. And my children, Jeff and Dani, who sent flowers and notes of encouragement throughout the writing of this book. They truly understood that my focus had temporarily shifted. And to my brother and sister-in-law, Peter and Susan, for their long distance support.

I am grateful for my friends who stood by me through the writing of this book. Susan Taylor, who believed in me before I believed in myself. Denise Newman, whose opinions I will always respect. Lamia Guarniere and Eileen Wasserman, my dear friends, who continually checked on my well-being.

Maureen R. Michelson, NewSage Press publisher extraordinare, taught me the true meaning of "the process." I learned from her jellybean-colored post-its that as my mind questions, my words must provide answers. I am grateful for her guidance, wisdom, and friendship. Her words, "Everyone is a first time author, once," will play in my mind forever.

Cindy McKechnie was the first at NewSage Press to see my vision and feel my passion for this book. I am grateful that she trusted her inner voice. And Tracy Smith, whose final editing made the last turn "sweet." Thank you for your honesty, openness, and humor.

Special thanks to Lloyd D. Pilch, D.V.M., and Philip S. Kennedy, D.V.M., who kept Kodiak alive that fateful day, making all of this possible. And to Treepeople for providing a nature sanctuary where I could hike with Kodiak and clear my head.

I am grateful to my guardian angel, who looked over my shoulder as this book came to life. And I thank my animals, past, present, and future. This book is written for them with the fervent hope that the world becomes a safer, healthier, and more loving place.

Bonnie S. Weintraub

CONTENTS

Conversations
with Animals

CARL HIBY

Lydia, 4, with her friend

– Chapter One –

THE GIFT OF
ANIMAL COMMUNICATION

Truly, as companions, friends, equals, in oppor-
tunities of self-expression, they unfold to me the
dignity of creation, and their joy smiles the
blessings of St. Francis.

— HELEN KELLER

I am an animal communicator or, if you prefer, an animal
psychic. Simply put, I talk to animals. It does not make a difference whether it's a horse, a dog, a dolphin, or an iguana, I
talk to them all.

What is most amazing to me is not the fact that I have conversations with many different species, but rather that as an adult
I was once a true skeptic. There was a time when I laughed at the
thought of humans and animals communicating with one another—until it was proven to me with my own animal. As a child I had
known that humans could talk with animals, but I had forgotten it.
Now I no longer laugh or roll my eyes because I am convinced—
without a doubt—that communication between animals and
humans exists.

The method I use to accomplish this wonder is nonverbal communication. "Picture talking" is the natural form of communication we instinctively use from the time we are born until we begin speaking verbally. But this ability deteriorates once a child enters school. I believe that with an open mind, and practice, it is not difficult to reclaim this ability and hone it into a skill.

Beatrice Lydecker, the renowned animal communicator, was my mentor. It was she who taught me the five guidelines she developed for successful communication with animals. The guidelines are: *emotions, perspective, time, positive terms,* and *discipline.* Throughout the book I will discuss how I apply these guidelines, and as they become more familiar, the process will seem less mysterious and perhaps, even more magical.

As I look back on my life I have always gravitated toward animals in hopes of knowing them better, never imagining the incredible journey that was about to unfold. In my "heart of hearts," I always knew that all living beings shared some existing form of communication. My first reaction upon meeting Beatrice was that of disbelief. Now, there are people who react this way to me. They emphatically declare that communication between human and animal is bogus. My own fear stemmed from the fact that I just didn't believe that something like this was even possible. I was fearful that I might be judged as a less than adequate caregiver to the animals in my life. Also, I was worried about the possibility of the horses with whom I worked being forced to do tasks not of their nature, while their complaints were falling on deaf ears! Now, it is my turn to listen and feel other people's fears about animal communication and open a door to greater understanding.

But beyond what I have learned from Beatrice, I have been educated by the animals themselves. They are my true teachers. I share a deep respect and love for them and continue to learn from them daily. The experiences animals have shared with me have changed my life. I want to share these lessons with you, and perhaps they may change your life, too.

My work with animals reinforces my belief in the powerful connection that weaves together humans, animals, and the universe we share. Through my experiences with animals I have been touched and blessed. As I see it, animals have been sent here by God to be our teachers, our therapists, and our healers. This has been proven to me time and again. When I communicate with animals, I am a silent observer. The words are not my own, but rather the animal's spirit talking to my higher self. Each time this phenomenon takes place I am humbled. It is this, and the stories in my soul that I wish to share in *Conversations with Animals*.

More than fifteen years ago I began an independent career as an animal communicator. The years of training and practical experience prepared me for the challenge. As the days passed, and the weeks turned into months and then into years, I began to accumulate a vast number of letters—some written to me prior to phone consultations and some follow-up notes from clients letting me know how things were progressing after communicating with their animal. Each encounter taught me something, and I treasured each letter. Once in awhile there was a letter that was so powerful—either because it moved me to tears or made me laugh out loud—that I could not shake it from my mind. These letters were put in a sturdy, plain cardboard box for a time when I could write a book. The box continued to swell with stories. I turned my wish for a book over to the universe, knowing that when it was the right time my book would be born.

Several years ago I received a telephone call from a new client, Bonnie Weintraub. She was calling about her dog, Kodiak, who urgently needed help. As a last resort Bonnie turned to me. When Bonnie called she was a confirmed skeptic. Yet, she kept an open mind. From the first conversation, I recognized that Kodiak, a beautiful black Standard Poodle, was a cherished animal. However, I never imagined he would have an ongoing role in my life. Ultimately, as events unfolded, it became clear that Kodiak's purpose was to bring Bonnie and me together to write this book. Kodiak recovered from a life-threatening situation as a result of my communicating with him, and Bonnie became my trusted friend in the process.

As time went on, I shared with Bonnie my desire to write a

book. She immediately dubbed this my "fundamental dream" and re-named my cardboard box the "box of dreams." It is Bonnie who writes this book with me because she has become my facilitator, just as I am the facilitator for the animals. She is able to "get in my head" just as I am able to get into the head and body of the animal with whom I am speaking. Together we tell of my experiences as an animal communicator and share with you the animals' stories and their lessons.

Bonnie and Kodiak

Fortunately, I have maintained my childhood fascination with animals and my ability to talk to them. My parents and family friends were open minded and accepted my uncanny ability as quite natural and matter of fact. There were no disapproving messages from the adults in my life that this could not be so. The stories I have been told of a little Lydia running around and declaring, "the dog said this," or "the horse said that," make me smile.

In truth, most of my childhood memories are hazy. Yet, when I recall an incident that involved an animal, the memory has a clarity and an intensity unlike any other. The colors, the sounds, the smells, all roll together and for a brief moment—even as an adult today—I am back in tune with the memory and the animal.

Every day my mother and I would venture, hand in hand, into the most precious part of the day. Mother called it our nature walk, our time together. As we left our property and headed down the bumpy gravel road, my eyes stretched across the landscape of rural Connecticut with its endless pastures neatly outlined with wooden split-rail fences.

At three years old, I was able to stick my head between the fence rails and greet my friends who lived in the pastures. I chatted with the horses, the donkeys, the cows, and the occasional dog who met us at the fence to remind us that protecting the property is a most important job. The dog might have been two to three feet away and my mother, never having been raised around animals, would warn, "Not too close." She was protective and somewhat fearful, but somehow I was able to pull her close to the fence and convince her that I must touch the cows and horses and dogs. She looked on in amazement as her independent toddler invited a horse to come over and talk. The conversations and questions, befitting a child, were simple. With my limited vocabulary, I called out to them and asked, "Are you happy? How are you feeling?" Most often I insisted, "Come say hi to me!"

Always, I felt comfortable talking to my animal friends. We enjoyed a mutual curiosity and my questions were politely asked with loving consideration. With each animal I encountered, I made eye contact. However, what I got back from the animals were neither words that they spoke, nor words that I heard in my head. Instead, I felt in my body a singular, intense emotion equivalent to *I'm happy—I'm sad—I'm hungry*. One single thought, one issue, one emotion is what I received from the animal. Perhaps that was all I was able to handle as a child. But I felt the animal's emotion—it came through the strongest. This, I believe, is what eventually led to my empathy and undoubtedly my ability to see through the eyes of the animals, and understand their perspective. However, now as an adult I realize that animals are capable of deep emotions, and are not just focused on food, water, or physical comforts.

If an animal did not come over to me I accepted the decision and tried not to act too disappointed. A cow might have communicated, *I'm busy eating—I see you*, and that's how it went. Communicating with animals seemed natural. And if they didn't want to speak to me that seemed okay, too.

Once my brother was born, the walks continued year-round, with my mother pushing a carriage, and I assisted her at three and one-half years old. Fortunately for me, there was little else to do in this rustic setting. Taking long walks and drives, we explored wonders that the countryside kept secret. We discovered natural streams, ponds, and dense forest growth populated with fascinating residents.

Eventually we left my beloved Connecticut and moved to Staten Island, New York. I left behind the open countryside and the nature walks, but ahead lay the world of horses. Within weeks of settling into our new home I experienced my first pony ride. I was four years old and I was hooked! This became a weekend ritual. I became so proficient at pestering my father that he relented and took me to the stables every Saturday, faithfully, for what was termed, "the damn pony ride!" I rode round and round the ring for as many times as the dollar allowed, but it always ended too soon. Still, this was far better than sticking my hand through the fence in Connecticut and touching a horse for a moment!

My father may have complained, but like any proud dad he loved watching me "ride" and as my riding improved so did my pestering, which I prefer to think of today as the artful ability of negotiation. Although I became skilled at this method of arbitration, I remained a realist. A horse is what I truly wanted, but I asked for a dog. Ginger, a Collie, became our family dog. I gave thanks in prayer and to Lassie for accomplishing this miracle.

Although Ginger was my dog, she was also a family member. My mother took great pride in teaching Ginger tricks and since she had never owned an animal before she was thrilled with Ginger's abilities. Before long, our family became extremely attached to this loving ball of fur. With her sable and white coat, Ginger looked like Lassie, but without the white markings on her face she was different, which made her uniquely Ginger. She was a true house dog, and slept in my room—actually on my bed, every night. Ginger was my best friend, my confidant, and with her I experienced the close bond an animal and a human can share. Together, we played veterinarian and although thoroughly embarrassed, Ginger allowed me to bandage her from head to tail. She loved me unconditionally, and it was Ginger who knew my secrets, and at the end of the day listened to my school-day troubles. So Ginger, with her big wet kisses and dark soulful eyes, made her way into our home and hearts—where no other animal had gone before.

My communication with Ginger did not entail me asking explicit questions and receiving answers. Instead, our communicating was a daily and subtle knowing. Looking into the eyes of a loved animal speaks volumes. Even now, only once in a great while, will I get a blatant message from one of my own companion animals. Usually it would be an emergency situation such as, *The front door is open* or *You*

Lydia, 10, and Ginger

better check on the cat. More frequently the messages are likely to be subtle and gentle. Because we are family members, our communication is automatic to a large extent.

Ginger was seven years old when she unexpectedly died following surgery for an infected uterus. Ginger's death was the first profound loss I had faced. I have come to believe that things happen for a reason, but at that time, there was no reason that could have satisfied me or my family. Ginger's death affected me so significantly at eleven years old that today it is directly responsible for the way in which I deal with my clients' loss and grief.

I had never before felt such overwhelming pain, and anguish seared through me when I learned of Ginger's death. My mother also was completely lost without her daytime companion. Within two days of losing Ginger, my mother, the woman who had never owned an animal in her life before, declared she just could not live in a house without a Collie! She realized that no dog would replace Ginger, but remained adamant about getting another dog immediately. Perhaps she needed a Collie body around her.

Perhaps she yearned for a dog's energy. Whatever the reason, a dog had touched her life to such an extent that she wanted an animal to share in her life. Mother was aware that the void Ginger left would not be filled when a new dog joined our family. We did grieve for Ginger. Everyone's timing is different, and Mother's was faster than mine.

With great difficulty we found a Collie breeder out on Long Island. After a two-hour drive we arrived at what I remember as Collie heaven. Every size and every color of Collies wiggled and yipped around us. The kennel was immaculate and run by what I term an old-time breeder who took great care of the puppies. Selecting our pup was the easy part. Waiting the three weeks until she was permitted to leave with us was agony.

We named the dog, "Ginger the Second," very original indeed! On her AKC papers she was "Lydia's Ginger" and that was quite official. Of course, she answered to Ginger. I learned from Lydia's Ginger that no two dogs are alike, and each animal enters our lives with specific needs and gifts. My second Ginger was my companion from my early teen years through my mid-twenties. However, I never forgot the first Ginger who taught me the joy and companionship possible with an animal companion.

Aside from Ginger, the animal that consumed my life was the horse. I progressed from getting pony rides as a child to giving pony rides as a teenager. Every Saturday I would oversee the pony rides as excited children rode them round and round the ring. The incentive for doing this work was that once we were finished for the day, the owner would let the employees trot around on the ponies. That was our big thrill as well as our compensation.

I also worked as an assistant at pony parties. People would hire the pony for the day and the pony would be transported to the residence. The truck would pull up, the ramp let down, and the kids could be heard screaming with excitement, "Oh, the pony's here!" If the party was not too far away I was allowed to ride the pony all the way back to the stables. That was the ultimate joy! For me, happiness was synonymous with horses. I hung around the stable every spare minute, and proudly earned the title "barn rat." My parents were delighted to know that I was either at school or at the stables.

There were three ponies used for the parties: Patches, a brown-and-white pinto, and twins named Bonnie and Clyde. The twins were real characters, full of personality. Bonnie was a sweet, feminine chestnut, while Clyde was black and quite handsome. Clyde was also a comedian. He knew how to take off his bridle. Clyde would stick two ears up, then one ear would move and the bridle would slide, fall off to the side, and end up hanging around his neck. I knew when he was planning to do this just by the way he looked at me. While working with Clyde in particular, I realized that I could actually put myself in the animal's frame of mind and sense how it felt to be him, and how it felt to be doing what was asked of him. For the longest time, I assumed that my ability to sense what an animal was going to do or wanted was responsible for my unique compatibility with animals. I often overheard comments about my "having a way with animals" but I never thought much about it. To me, this was just me.

Because I spent so much time at the stables, I became very aware of Dusty, an old draft horse. He was semi-retired, and no one spent time with him. Dusty became my pet project. I was warned that although Dusty was neither mean nor aggressive, a kid would never have the patience needed to reach him. I accepted this challenge and proceeded to prove them wrong. Dusty's coat and mane were a mess and slowly he let me touch him and brush him. As he came to know me he let me pick up his hooves—something that could be quite dangerous if a horse does not trust you. I brought him treats and he began to look forward to my visits and came to expect me.

One day I felt that something was terribly wrong with Dusty and I told the stable owner. The owner listened intently to what I had to say and what I felt. He certainly did not discourage me and seemed open to any input because he had witnessed my connection with this animal. Dusty ultimately stopped eating. I spent many hours with him until he got so sick he was put to sleep. Dusty taught me patience, and I gave him love.

In time I graduated from pony parties to accompanying groups on horseback trail rides. Some days there were as many as thirteen or fourteen people in our charge, each having paid fifteen dollars for an hour-long trail ride. Looking back, I am stunned by the responsibility we assumed considering some riders had never before been in a saddle. This certainly would not happen now with the liability concerns in our society. Perhaps it was a time of innocence all around. We were as happy as could be sitting in a saddle upwards of ten hours a day. Again, there was no pay involved, it was just being able to ride. We took no lunch time and if we had to go to the bathroom, we would jump off and run in the bushes. During this time of my life, all that mattered was being on a horse and riding!

The adage seems to apply here: the busiest people are those who seem to find the time to do more. At this time, I also began volunteering at the Staten Island Zoo. My job was to mix the food and assist the keepers at the children's zoo. As a high school sophomore I loved the work. Ultimately, this led to summer work at the petting zoo, where volunteers prepared lectures and demonstrations and were responsible for monitoring the children. Among the animals at the petting zoo was a llama, Larry. He was the first llama I had ever known. He had a white face and a dark-brown body. Just being around Larry was wonderful. Most of all, I loved how he hummed. I often would sit in his pen quietly, listen to his hum as if it were a mantra, and feel peaceful and rested. When I was with him everything else seemed to fade away and disappear. My time with Larry and his "llama presence" was the first experience I had with any kind of meditating.

This particular zoo had been built at the turn of the century, consequently the enclosures were rather small and substandard. I began to question whether it was proper to have big animals in small cages. Conscious of the animals' reality and feelings, I put myself in the animals' place to see from their perspective. My observations were personal and as my spiritual growth continued I sensed that the animals were aware and capable of feelings.

Perhaps others recognized these feelings as well, for when the zoo's extensive renovation program began, great efforts were made to accurately recreate large natural wildlife settings.

After high school I moved away to attend Delhi Agriculture Technical College in upstate New York that specialized in Animal Science. Two years later I graduated as a "vet tech," or an animal nurse. I continued to work full time at the small animal clinic that employed me during college summers. Life seemed pretty good; however, when things are nearly perfect, a twist is usually thrown in to shake things up. My car was hit by a drunk driver as I returned home from work early one evening. From this experience I clearly saw how much I leaned on my family and my animal companions for healing and energy. While I recovered from the accident, I had time to reach a decision and announce to my family that I was ready to move "far away" to the state next door. New Jersey would become my home as soon as I recovered.

In New Jersey, I held two jobs to make ends meet. I worked as a tech at an animal hospital for eight hours during the day and at night I worked at a horse farm for seven hours. It was a crazy life. I wanted so much to be with horses again that I was willing to do whatever was needed. Since my responsibilities with the horses ended at ten at night I was given an apartment over the stables. I had full range of the care, gear, and grooming of the horses in my charge, but my favorite job was feeding them supper every night. Sometimes I would feed all forty-five horses, turn out the light in the barn, and sit in the hallway listening. The horses would munch, snort, and talk to one another. Any horse lover knows the sweet sound of a horse eating and knowing they feel truly content.

My responsibilities at the horse barn were significant. The horses stabled at this facility competed at influential shows such as Devon and Madison Square Garden, which are considered two of the premiere events of the East Coast horse world. The financial investment to prepare a horse for competition riding in Hunters and Jumpers divisions was substantial indeed. I had come a long way from the pony rides at birthday parties.

Thirteen of these spectacular animals were entrusted to me,

and most were known as the wild ones of the barn because of their difficult personalities. The reason that the high maintenance horses (demanding both emotionally and physically) were placed in my care was that I had the patience needed to deal with them. It was flattering to be thought of in such terms, but it was a challenge.

One of the horses I cared for was Buffy, a magnificent horse, but a youngster in a big body. He was a prankster at heart. It was impossible to give him a bath until I let him hold the hose above my head and shower me first. Another horse, Thomas, was dangerous and kicked without warning. Twice he had come close to killing the groom working on him. Thomas usually kicked while his legs were being wrapped or "set up" after a training session, a common procedure used to prevent sports injuries. Sadly, it was rumored that Thomas did not like people because he had experienced abuse by a previous owner.

Peter, a gray horse at least sixteen hands high, was unreasonably frightened when he was covered with blankets at night. He was layered with several blankets and this ordeal took two hours to complete. It was a sad sight as Peter stood fearfully shaking because he once had been scared so badly. Most likely a past owner or groom had gotten the surcingle (strap) caught underneath Peter's legs. This would cause a horse to feel trapped, almost strait-jacketed. Peter could not stand the strap on his belly, and he was afraid his legs would get tangled up. Peter was purchased with this quirk, and although his new owners tried, they never found out for sure what caused this peculiar behavior.

My apartment above the clubroom overlooked the indoor arena. My dog Ginger, and my recently adopted cat, Jesse, lived with me. One evening after finishing chores, I overheard the announcement, "This woman from California is going to come and talk to the animals!!!" I immediately thought, *Please—Give me a break!* Fortunately, I kept my skepticism to myself. Two days later the owner of the barn mentioned quite casually that a woman from California was coming to talk to the animals. When I heard this, I thought, *Right, I don't think so.*

People at the barn began talking about this woman's visit. Never had I witnessed such excitement. The buzz around the stables was that this was going to be "so cool." The animal communicator was Beatrice Lydecker. She arrived in a motor home with eight German Shepherds in tow. My initial thought was, *The dog and pony show is here!* Grateful for my morning job, I ran off not giving this woman another thought.

But that afternoon when I returned to the stables, the atmosphere was still charged. The murmurs were a reaction to the unsettling and astonishing information gleaned from the twenty horses Beatrice conversed with. She had spoken to Peter, relaying the fact that he was frightened by blankets. When I heard that information, my immediate reaction was to blow her off. Beatrice had taken me off guard with her accuracy and I felt uneasy, almost scared. There were forty-five stabled horses needing care. I had more important things to do than stand around and watch "the animal psychic" and listen to the stories of the newly impressed crowd.

Early Sunday morning Beatrice moved her motor home into the indoor arena and proceeded to exercise her eight Shepherds. Walking up the aisle, peering through the glass into the indoor arena, I found myself staring at the eight dogs. All dog eyes were intently focused on one lone cat pressed up against a little ledge. I recognized Bijou, a barn cat, and felt her panic. Beatrice was unaware of the situation since she was at the far end of the barn consulting with a horse, so it was up to me to do something. I pushed the door open and walked into the arena right past the eight dogs, saying in a very stern voice, "Well, that's not polite—you're not being very nice." I picked the cat up and with great authority strode out of the arena. Bijou's hair was all puffed out, and I sensed that just seconds ago, she feared for her life. Bijou was very thankful for my rescue.

Still regaining my composure I was startled when Joella, my trainer, grabbed me as I exited the arena and pushed me against the wall. Chastising and questioning my sanity at the same time, she yelled, "I can't believe you did that. You just walked in there with all those dogs. Didn't you think you'd be bitten?" I hadn't even thought about it. There had been no time, I tried to explain. I just did what had to be done.

That day, Beatrice worked with the horses until dusk. Several times I caught her looking at me and I responded by rolling my eyes and saying something under my breath like, *This is a bunch of nonsense!* I must have embodied the ultimate skeptic! Finally, she cornered me and asked if I had been the one who walked into the arena with her dogs present. I nodded and most definitely made another face. Questioning me further, she asked, "Weren't you nervous?" "No," I replied, drifting back to the scene, still fresh in my mind.

Her next question, "Do you believe in what I do?" took me completely off guard. I stammered something unintelligible, thinking any response would satisfy her. But when I turned to leave, her words trailed after me. Beatrice persisted, "How did you feel comfortable walking in with all of those dogs?" Then she added, "By the way, I spoke to all of the horses that you take care of and each one told me that you already talk to them—so why don't you believe me?" Not knowing how to answer, I just prayed to be left alone. No luck. Instead, Beatrice then asked, "Do you have an animal here?" Next, came an invitation to dinner. Deciding that it was pointless to fight her tenacity I agreed to join her for dinner. I ran upstairs to grab a picture of Ginger who happened to be spending the weekend with my mom in Staten Island.

In truth I wanted to give Beatrice the opportunity to explain what she did. When I hesitantly entered the enclosed arena and headed toward her motor home, the sight of her dogs swirling around the vehicle reminded me of a swarm of bees. She cooked something quickly, then turned her attention to the photo of Ginger. I was trying to humor her, still skeptical of her abilities. Beatrice asked me my dog's name and where the dog was physically located at that moment. Barely uttering the words, "Ginger and Staten Island," she began to give me detail after detail about my father, my mother, my brother, and my family's relationship with this loving animal. Stunned, my mouth dropped open.

Beatrice looked at me intensely, still uncertain whether or not my mind had been changed.

After our visit I was still confused. I did not understand why Beatrice singled me out. The horses had told her that I talked to them, and Beatrice also watched me with the dogs, but those were only two incidents. Perhaps being the last skeptic, the last hold-out at the stables, she felt compelled to push me beyond my doubts. The next day Beatrice handed me her address, and said, "If you ever come to California, look me up." She then called to her dogs, loaded them on board, and drove off to her next destination.

As her motor home faded into the distance, I reflected for a long time on what had happened. I was amazed that Beatrice told me accurate details about Ginger even though the dog was not in front of her. And then it hit me and when it did, I was astounded. Beatrice did this from a photograph! For weeks, I thought a great deal about our first encounter, and that she tried to convince me that I was *already* using communication techniques. I never discredited her, but I didn't feel confident in my abilities either.

Beatrice's "reading" on Ginger remained a pivotal point in what would become my work as an animal communicator. Over time I became more conscious and attentive to the process I used to speak to the animals. I communicated verbally, which certainly was elementary. Trusting my gut became more comfortable, and without realizing it, I began to depend on my instincts. The moment I accepted my ability to see from the animals' perspective and feel how life felt to them—was the instant the connection occurred.

The need to expand my experience with animals led me to The Cat Practice, an all-feline hospital in New York City. Toward the end of the first year, a mailing arrived from Beatrice announcing her plans to visit New York City for work. She also wanted to teach a class in animal communication while she was in town. This was the perfect opportunity for me to learn a new way to better assist the veterinarians in handling and treating the clinic animals. So, I set up a group of ten people intrigued with the topic. But in typical East Coast fashion the worst snowstorm of the season dropped three feet of snow, crippling the city, and limiting the number attending the class to those who could walk there. With five students present, Beatrice taught the techniques she uses to talk to the animals.

At the end of the class Beatrice encouraged us to practice the techniques we had learned. Most importantly, the class validated that others can communicate with animals. Perhaps because of my education steeped in science, and thinking clinically, I questioned if it was possible to communicate with animals. The intimate setting and the individualized attention allowed me to observe others and make up my own mind. After Beatrice returned to sunny California, I had a gnawing feeling that somehow I had changed. Blessed with acute intuition and now firmly accepting that animals could communicate with humans, I was totally unprepared for what lay ahead.

Winter continued its harsh pounding with one fierce snow storm blending into the next. Bone-chilling temperatures refused to abate. My personal life sent a chill through me as well. I was not ready to make a lifetime commitment to my boyfriend or to marriage. And I was struggling with the possibility of a career change. The warmth of California and its dream summoned me and I went.

With starry-eyed enthusiasm, I flew to California to scope out the job situation and scheduled interviews with individual veterinarians. During a meeting with Beatrice, she offered to accept me as her student if I was interested. When I returned to New York, my head was spinning and I decided that whatever happened was meant to be. When I got home, the answering machine light was blinking. There was a job offer with a Los Angeles vet hospital that began in two weeks. It took me four days to drive from New York to California, and the remaining time was spent finding a place to live and settling into a new home.

During the next four years I worked in veterinary clinics while I studied animal communication with Beatrice. In the beginning, I was invited to follow her around as she worked with numerous horses at ranches and at barns. I was expected to practice talking to each animal and Beatrice would check my precision throughout the day. Quite often I was hesitant and felt uncomfortable reporting my "findings," certain that the information was inaccurate. If it had not been for Beatrice's belief in my abilities, I never would have succeeded. In my early twenties, I was not filled with an abundance of confidence and self-esteem. Beatrice was relentless, and constantly pushed me. I sought her approval, and tried to please her. Her faith in my capability never wavered, although I continually questioned myself. Beatrice, it seemed, was correct most of the time—no matter what species of animal—no matter what problem. Imagine being trained by a teacher who was seldom plagued by error. It was not easy for me, the protégée, but I stuck with it because I was hooked—and Beatrice was unyielding.

My responsibilities progressed along with my accuracy. By the time Beatrice traveled to Holland (her book, *What the Animals Tell Me*, had been translated into Dutch) I had taken over the care of her animals and to my delight was encouraged to work with her clients. Her trust boosted my confidence and the "pictures" I was getting were coming faster and more easily. I made every effort to be accurate but learned to accept that I could and would make a mistake or mistranslate a message from an animal. Thankfully, this rarely occurred. Toward the end of my apprenticeship we traveled across the United States in two motor homes, covering 19,000 miles in nine months, making personal appearances along the way.

The exposure to the media and the diverse experiences were priceless. I learned how to handle myself with aplomb in a variety of different situations, from guest appearances on television to lecturing at a podium staring into hundreds of faces. All of this prepared me to go solo as an animal communicator.

Lydia with a client

– *Chapter Two* –

ANIMALS
AND THEIR EMOTIONS

*Animals are such agreeable friends. They ask no
questions, they pass no criticisms.*

– GEORGE ELIOT

H ave you ever experienced a moment when you thought
your pet was trying to send you a message, struggling to
communicate? Perhaps your dog thrust out his paw
repeatedly, or paced back and forth whining, or just stared at you—
trying to "tell" you something. Possibly your cat kept meowing and
jumping up in your lap. If you have shared such an experience with
your pet, did you get a sense of what your animal was trying to
say? Did the message seem too innocent or too "off the wall" and
cause you to doubt where the information was coming from?
Maybe you wondered if your imagination was working overtime?
I believe the information we receive in these situations must be
coming from the animal.

In one sense emotions are difficult to pinpoint because they
are intangible. But in actuality, a message emanating from emotion is no more difficult to interpret than the visual message that
identifies an object like a dog's blue food bowl. If you allow yourself to be open to communicating with your pet, chances are that

you will connect with your animal's emotions and move beyond your doubt. Pet owners get past this wall of doubt when they follow a gut feeling—a message from the heart—or a sixth sense. This trust becomes validation they can accept.

I have often been plagued with self-doubt when communicating with animals, unsure of whether or not I should acknowledge the validity of the information that came to me. This occurred most often during my training as an animal communicator. Fortunately, during these episodes of doubt, an animal and a situation materialized—making it possible for me to believe and trust the messages. At first I thought these events to be mere coincidences, but looking back, I see that my life has been filled with synchronicity.

One powerful incident that became a catalyst in helping me trust and be receptive, happened while I was working as a vet technician. My duties as an animal nurse were basic, and daily, I was immersed in the world of science and medicine. I worked among x-ray machines, stainless steel tables, and antiseptic smells, but I continued to draw on the knowledge acquired in Beatrice Lydecker's class, "How to Talk to the Animals." One day a petite, cream-colored, long-haired cat was rushed into the veterinary hospital. The cat had difficulty giving birth to her litter and the owner confirmed one kitten had died. We needed to determine if any kittens were left in the womb or lodged in the birth canal, which would have explained the cat's distress. The vet requested an x-ray.

Taking x-rays had become my specialty and I was often able to accomplish this procedure without using an anesthetic because I gained the trust and cooperation of my animal patient. This cat was weak and exhausted. I placed her gently on the examining table confident that she would remain still.

Completely focused on preparing the x-ray, my concentration was jolted when I heard, *Did my kitten die?* Presuming someone had spoken these words, I looked up but realized I was alone. It never occurred to me to look at the cat. Again, I heard the words, *Did my kitten die?* My rational mind dismissed the question.

Pressed for time, I continued to set up the x-ray machine. The question came again, but this time with a sense of urgency and a mild annoyance, *Is my kitten dead? What happened to her?* Simultaneously, the cat and I looked at each other. Our eyes locked. I could not pull away. She concentrated on sending me the message—the message she expected me to receive. Mesmerized, I heard myself answer verbally, "Yes, your kitten is dead." The cat turned away sighing, grief stricken. No one had told the cat that one of her kittens had died. A short while later, I returned the cat to her owner and retreated to the treatment room, alone. My mind raced, trying to make sense of exactly *what* had just happened.

Up until then I had never experienced an animal being that precise. Automatically, I put myself in the cat's position, trying to see life from her perspective. This was my emotional side. My rational mind was still questioning whether this was the proper way to deal with a dilemma. I never conceived that something so definite, so clear, so powerful, could be sent by a four-footed creature, and received by me, a human being.

There had to be something more, something I did not yet grasp. Perhaps the cat in the veterinary hospital was an animal messenger, sent to get through to me. It was as if the cat was saying, *Hey pay attention! This is really happening! Just be open!* The cat's message echoed in my memory as I repeated to myself, *Is my kitten dead?*

As a child I automatically trusted the feelings and messages I received from animals. Since then, I have learned, once again, to trust what the animals tell me. Many times, I have experienced a wide range of emotions with my own pets because I treat them as family members, giving them the same love and respect most people reserve for humans.

Experience has taught me some basic concepts that animals perceive and feel with their human owners. For example, many animals think:

You're my mom.
You take care of me.
I expect you to be there.

Other animals think:

I take care of you.

If you feed me—that's great!

These are gut emotions. Continuously, I am amazed and humbled by animals who reveal a variety of emotions that run deep. Perhaps my openness is directly responsible for an animal feeling comfortable enough to share powerful feelings. Every consultation with an animal enlightens my understanding of their capacity for emotional depth. One of my early clients offered me a valuable lesson in animal emotions.

On my first solo barn visit, I met a horse who would teach me a lifetime lesson in communicating with animals. On a crisp autumn day I entered the white iron gates of Windswept Stables, a magnificent spread for horses. The owner of the stables, Anita, is an easy-going woman in her forties. She met me wearing English breeches and riding boots. Anita immediately confided that my visit to her stables to "talk" to her horses was fulfilling a childhood dream. As is often the case, her warm welcome eased my apprehension.

Anita ushered me into the barn and introduced me to my day's first client, a gray gelding. The consultation went smoothly and Anita was surprised and delighted by my accuracy.

The next stall was home to a mare and her three-month old colt. She had been purchased while in foal and Anita wanted to know more about her previous history. I described the baby's personality, as well as his desire to do dressage. (Dressage is the discipline where the horse and rider learn a series of patterns and move with fluidity. At the higher levels of competition, dressage is a beautiful and graceful event often described as "ballet on horseback.") The young colt learned about dressage from his mom, the mare. Anita was in awe as I explained that the baby colt had actually received visual images about dressage from his mother. The colt therefore understood the intricate details of dressage as well as the more basic concept of his job—to be ridden by people.

After I completed these readings, I was escorted across the aisle and introduced to Robin, a woman who had a dual role as assistant trainer and groom. Scanning the barn, I was immediately impressed with the meticulous conditions in which these animals lived. A peacefulness and calm were noticeable as a result of such proper order. Robin took great pride in my acknowledging her dedication.

At the edge of the next client's stall I stopped and did what I always do, mentally ask the horse permission to enter. Daniel was a huge, gorgeous, healthy fourteen-year old horse. He had his back to me, which was unusual, and, for some reason, I had an odd feeling. Most animals face me and are excited to talk. This was different. Without waiting for an answer, Robin ushered me in. As I entered Daniel's stall, a wave of remorse and grief swept over me. I wondered where these feelings were coming from. Daniel slowly looked over his shoulder at me, letting me know by the feeling sent that he was very offended that I was in his stall. I mentally asked him, *What's wrong?* No response. I asked him again, *What's wrong?* Again, I began to feel his emotions of grief, fear, and anger. From the depth of his despair, it finally surfaced, and Daniel said, *My life is over!*

Feeling rattled, I told Robin that Daniel refused to converse any further, and that all he would share is the thought, *My life is over!* Robin pleaded with me to make an effort to continue. *Shouldn't I respect his wishes?* I asked myself. *Was I prepared for this?* This scenario was not something I had planned. After a minute I gently asked Daniel again, *What's wrong?* A fragment of information mixed with raw emotion washed over me as I felt his pain. Daniel was grieving, but for whom? A horse? A person? "Robin," I whispered, "someone has died." It was at this point Robin filled in the blanks about Daniel's original owner, Chet. Chet had a long-term, chronic heart problem and had a fatal heart attack two days earlier. Robin sensed that Daniel knew his owner was gone, even though Chet and Daniel had not physically been together at the time of his death, nor had anyone told Daniel. Robin observed that since Chet's death, Daniel had seemed depressed.

Robin then told me that Chet had bequeathed Daniel to her,

and that she would be taking care of him. Pausing for a moment, I looked back at Daniel, his head drooping, and realized that he was unaware of the arrangements made on his behalf. Again, Daniel said, *My life is over. My dad's not here, I don't want to live anymore.* It was so overwhelming emotionally that I couldn't ask him basic questions. Then Daniel told me, *I don't want to talk to you. My life is over.* I walked out of his stall and said to Robin, "I'm going to see another horse. Why don't you talk to him and tell him what's going on?" Unsure of what to do, Robin asked me, "How?" I explained, "Verbally tell him your plans for the future. Second, let him know you are his owner now. Tell him his life isn't over. Finally, let him know it's okay to grieve." I left to meet with another horse, reassuring them both that I would return. While I was gone, Robin told Daniel that Chet wanted her to take care of him now and love him.

Twenty minutes later I returned to Daniel's stall, and as I walked through the door he turned around to face me. The first message he sent me was the question, *Is she telling me the truth?* I visualized from Daniel what Robin had said to him. The feeling I got back from the horse was, *She's my owner now and we're going to be doing the same things that my dad and I did. Is this true?* That's all he wanted to know. Robin reassured Daniel with her verbal response, "Yes, that's exactly what's going to happen."

Once Daniel felt reassured, he wanted to verify all the information he had been given by Robin. Wanting to trust, yet needing further reassurance, he asked me again. I sent him a simple message, *Yes, that is what will happen.*

I turned and walked out of the barn, my emotions and senses heightened by the experience. Aware of the gravel crunching beneath my feet, it felt good to take a deep breath, inhale the cool autumn air, and look up at the brilliant blue sky to clear my head. As I walked to my van I wondered, *How did that horse know that his owner died?* I never doubted that horses had deep feelings, but I had never experienced anything like this before. I was humbled. Daniel remains the only animal who did not want to "talk" to me.

After that meeting with Daniel, I kept replaying his words, *My life is over.* It was so final. *I will die of a broken heart.* The hopeless message was such a paradox to the visual image of Daniel. He was a pampered animal, a highly fit Thoroughbred. But all I kept hearing over and over again was his message, *My life is over. I have nothing to live for—nothing.* I never doubted what Daniel told me since I received his message in my head and felt his anguish in my heart. I literally "felt" the truth in my body, and "thought" the truth in my head.

What I witnessed with Daniel was in direct conflict with the scientific knowledge I had acquired in college. I learned that anthropomorphizing animals is an attempt to ascribe human attributes, such as emotions, to them. There has been no satisfactory way to prove to science that animals perceive the same emotions humans feel, or at least that is what I thought back then. Since Daniel, all of my thinking about this has been turned upside down and transformed.

The relationship between Chet and Daniel was a special union based upon their working together. Most people see horses being ridden and perceive only dominance. It is not. It is total cooperation, but the general public doesn't know that. Most observers assume the horse would not cooperate without the metal bit in his mouth. That is not true. Daniel and Chet were a perfect example of a balanced relationship between a horse and a human. My experience with Daniel taught me that an animal's inner feelings are far more complex than I had previously realized. Once again I had to acknowledge that animals' intuitive abilities to heal themselves and humans are far more powerful than I had imagined. Even now with years of experience in the field of animal communication, I still reflect back on certain early messages from special animal teachers: *Is my kitten dead? My life is over!*

Most animal lovers accept that dogs and cats go through a mourning period when a family member dies, whether it is another pet or a human being. This holds true for any animal species. Emotions and intelligence of an animal should not be judged by humans. Animals are as individual as people and motivations for animals are as varied as those for humans. We need to try to see the world from their perspective. That's what talking to animals tells me. If you can imagine this, you will have a far better idea of the motivation behind the animal.

Animals are not always motivated by food, praise, or a reward. Sometimes animals respond out of the goodness of their hearts with no thought of compensation. Other animals may behave in certain ways simply because of fear of punishment. And some animals, like people, are ego-driven. The best example of this is the darling pup known as the princess of the house who sends out the message, *Just take care of me. I am here to be pampered.* Other animals are active participants or what I think of as guardian angels—empathetic, selfless, and motivated simply by a kind word. There are also those animals motivated primarily by instinct. For instance, the genetic tendency that drives the herding instinct is so powerfully ingrained that it is impossible for the animal to disconnect from it.

Many times people have told me that they were drawn to an animal because of the animal's eyes. Horse people, in particular, talk about picking a particular horse because she had a "very soft eye." Similarly, pet owners tell stories of picking a cat or dog because "he looked up at me with these loving, needy eyes." I believe the eyes are the gateway to the soul, and this can be the first point of connection that, in time, will lead to a deeper "feeling connection."

Animals have an innate ability to give companionship and love unconditionally. This is why I think animals are here. Some people have already learned this. Perhaps by accident an animal may have been responsible for a turning point in your life. "I wasn't planning on getting a dog, but he was so adorable." Or, "I never liked cats, but I was at the supermarket and this kid was giving away kittens." Or, how about this one? "I went to the pound with my friend, and here was this dog going, *Uh, excuse me, you're taking me home. I don't know what happened, I just sort of went out of myself and did it!* Sometimes you have to trust your first gut instinct, as well as the "gut feeling" you may be picking up from the animal.

The feeling connection between animals and humans can be a

healing power for humans. Similarly, I believe that's how we pick our best friends. The people we choose to be part of our life are the people who allow us to be ourselves. How do you feel about them? How do you feel about yourself when you are with them? Most likely, you feel safe and accepted. More often than not, your close friends are open and honest, and have a great capacity for accepting you the way you are.

⌐

A grassy hillside on a client's ranch was the site of another important and influential animal lesson. During this group consultation I met Melinda and her black Lab mix, Dreamer, whom she had rescued from the pound. The dog arrived at the consultation wearing a full muzzle. Melinda's explanation was that Dreamer did not get along with other dogs. She said Dreamer was aggressive and usually went after other animals. Dreamer sat next to me and as I turned my attention to her and began to communicate, she put her head on my lap and looked up at me. The first emotional message Dreamer sent was, *I have to wear this muzzle because my mom is worried about me.*

Dreamer understood that humans saw her as a liability, capable of hurting another animal or a person. I asked Dreamer questions about the pound and how she got there. With mental pictures she showed me images of abuse. She was chained and beaten. A previous owner had hit Dreamer on the head. As a result of the head trauma, Dreamer had suffered some kind of brain damage. She accepted wearing the muzzle because she knew there was a slight chance that she could bite someone, and if this occurred her owner would be in serious trouble.

In Dreamer's case, I sensed brain damage existed by the dog's response to my question. I have recognized this in other animals as well. If, when I ask a question, the animal responds immediately, I can deduce that the brain functions normally. The answer is clear and the response quick. When an animal has any kind of brain damage, the answer just does not come through properly or sometimes it does not come through at all. In addition, I feel the animal's personality and strong emotions while trying to respond, *I know what I need to say but I can't make my body cooperate—or my mind cooperate.* The animal is well aware that the message is not being sent correctly. And as with a human stroke victim, I can feel the frustration. I also have felt the sensation and the pain of being hit in the head when I experienced the blow suffered by an abused animal and the aftermath of the painful migraine headache.

Dreamer told me that she knew at the pound that Melinda was going to adopt her and commented, *I don't know why she picked me from all the other animals.* Dreamer also knew she was going to be put to sleep that very day. With all the abuse and pain she had suffered, she was willing to be released from her body. When Melinda came to bail her out of the pound, Dreamer warned, *You don't know what you're getting yourself into! I am difficult. I am hard to take care of. I am a lot of work!* Melinda soon learned that the time investment in Dreamer would be substantial.

Dreamer told me she felt guilty for Melinda's change in lifestyle. People stopped visiting, and Melinda didn't entertain as much, in large part due to the dog's aggressive behavior. Melinda shared with me her reasons for choosing Dreamer. "I felt in my heart that something bad had happened to Dreamer. That's what I saw in her eyes, and that's why I rescued her. There were a lot of other dogs I was attracted to, but I knew I could help this one. I knew I could be with Dreamer and make her feel better." During the course of our conversation, the dog said, *I'm really so thankful. I didn't know people could be so nice.* Melinda wanted to know why Dreamer avoided having her head stroked. After sharing with her what Dreamer had conveyed to me, Melinda realized that for Dreamer a raised hand did not mean a stroke of love, but rather a blow.

While I talked with Dreamer and Melinda I began the healing process by sending visual pictures to Dreamer of people touching her and stroking her like a baby. She asked innocently, *Is that what people are supposed to do?* Dreamer had no pleasant memories of humans petting her. This consultation was filled with emotion and understandably, many of the clients sitting on the hillside, awaiting their appointments, began to cry. It never occurred to Dreamer that people could be as kind as her mom.

Melinda had been a teacher for Dreamer and showed the dog that people could be extraordinarily giving and caring. In turn, Melinda learned from Dreamer who taught her patience and commitment. Melinda was well aware that adopting Dreamer would be difficult, but could never have known *how* difficult. But with time, Dreamer learned to give love and willingly receive affection. Once again, I was touched and taught by the wisdom of a four-legged being.

As I turned to give my attention to the next client, someone nudged me. Melinda had taken the muzzle off Dreamer, and every person at the meeting was touching the dog. While human hands stroked Dreamer's head, she wagged her tail. The dog's entire demeanor had changed. The transformation was immediate, as though Dreamer had just finished a session in group therapy. A sizable dog who lived on the ranch, moved slowly up the hillside toward Dreamer. Dreamer remained calm. Sitting down along side each other, the two dogs had their first conversation.

Since that session. I have kept in touch with Melinda. Although Dreamer does not joyfully greet everyone, she no longer wears her muzzle on walks. Without the muzzle, Dreamer is not seen as a ferocious dog. Even her facial expression has softened. I feel blessed to have been a part of this metamorphosis.

Although I am usually empathetic with pet owners and their concerns, it is easier to remain controlled during a telephone consultation compared to a consultation that takes place in person. However, when the consultation is intense or personal, it may be impossible for me to hide my feelings whether the consultation happens over a telephone or occurs in person. In truth, I never know what pictures and emotions an animal will send me until the consultation is under way. I have learned to be open to the feelings, whatever they may be.

Willie, a Cocker Spaniel was one such animal who took me by surprise. At first glance he fit the image of the indulged pet—quite dapper dressed in his leather biker outfit. Nothing phases me, having seen people spend excessive amounts on their pets, but this outfit was extreme! The man who owned Willie was nicely dressed as well, so it seemed appropriate to expect that this consultation would provide fun and light entertainment. My assumption was wrong. Within moments of beginning the consultation, I was overcome with such a powerful feeling of love that my eyes teared up and a lump swelled in my throat. This emotional moment was captured by a television camera filming a segment for "48 Hours" that was aptly entitled "Pet Passion."

Immediately I could feel the sweet affection between Willie and his owner, Thomas. I later learned that at one time Thomas was homeless and lived out of his car, which he kept parked on the street adjacent to a park. During that time Thomas was down on his luck, and took odd jobs. If necessary he would hunt through garbage cans at the park looking for food. Swallowing his pride, Thomas resorted to pan handling only to feed Willie. There were days he collected enough change to buy only one burger, which he gave to his dog. Thomas was committed to taking care of Willie. When I communicated with Willie, he told me, *Thomas put my life first.*

During these hard times, Thomas gave Willie his word that they would always be together and some day, perhaps far in the future, they would share fun times. The promise was kept. Willie's twelfth birthday gift was a consultation with me. And the frivolous outfit was for fun. Willie enjoyed wearing it since he was the kind of dog who liked people enjoying him. It also meant that Willie's owner had made it back to a world where he could smile.

It never ceases to amaze me that I have been chosen to play the part of the facilitator, the mouthpiece for the animal in need. Once I understand an animal's motivation, then I am confident I can deal with the problem and make the animal feel whole. Many times it can be the conversation alone that makes an animal feel better. The simple fact that *their* feelings are being acknowledged and listened to can be healing for both the animal and the human.

Have you ever thought for a moment what life would be like if the animals were our caretakers? I have imagined this very possibility. In my opinion, humankind would be in far better shape since animals deal with important "basic life issues." These issues are the foundation of human and animal existence: food, shelter and clothing. In my view there are spiritual life issues as well. Included under this heading are unconditional love, nurturing, mutual respect, security, and safety.

Unfortunately, humans have become a community in which we often do not take responsibility for our actions. This turn of events disheartens me. As we have become adjusted to shutting off our emotions, we as a people have become comfortable throwing things away when they no longer have a use. Sadly, this attitude has trickled down to dealing with animals who are often discarded and disposed of without a second thought. Humans have become a species of takers, thinking first of "me, me, me." However, our awareness is beginning to swing back to caring for the earth. It has taken animals to move us beyond our selfishness.

Animals are real and true to themselves. "Being present" is their lesson to us. However, being present requires listening with one's whole self, giving one's full attention, living in the moment, and cherishing what you have now. Animals continue to demonstrate being in the moment. That is why time is not a factor. Time, from the first sundial to the current digital watch, is a human concept. Making a conscious decision to stop—to look—to hear—to feel—what is happening at the moment is the richest way to live life. This is the truest expression of self.

The sweetest gift the animals return to us is the ability to feel childlike again. When you reach a childlike quality, you are your "true self." There is no mask. There is no game. You are present in the moment with your feelings and all that you are.

I feel passionate about my work and creating a bridge that connects animals and humans. Ultimately, it is my hope that the link between a human and an animal companion will deepen with communication, bringing a new level of understanding to the relationship. As humans reconnect with animals, nature, and the earth, we will all be strengthened.

Kodiak

– *Chapter Three* –

DOG TALES

Dogs' lives are too short. Their only fault, really.

— CARLOTTA MONTEREY O'NEILL

M y co-author, Bonnie Weintraub, and I actually attribute our friendship, and ultimately, the writing of this book to Bonnie's dog Kodiak. Bonnie and I first met when Kodiak faced life-threatening circumstances that ultimately were resolved. The following is Bonnie's story of Kodiak.

⌐

It was Ground Hog's Day in 1994 when my journey to an unknown world began. Early that February morning while switching cars with my husband, something caused my Standard Poodle, Kodiak, to tumble into the swimming pool. Within minutes I found his black figure already partially submerged. Flashbacks of a blue-black tongue hanging out of his mouth still disturb my sleep, and the shock of jumping into icy water awakens me.

As I dragged Kodiak's limp body up the pool steps and placed him on the cement decking, overwhelming terror struck as I realized there was no life in this animal. Automatic pilot took over. Trained in CPR, I instinctively pried Kodiak's mouth open and tried to breathe life into him. Air escaped. Without thinking, I cupped my hand over his closed mouth and placed my mouth over his nose and began breathing, mouth to nose. Blow - two - three - stop. Blow - two - three - stop. Between breaths I pleaded, "Don't you die! Breathe for me! Don't you die!" And by the grace of God he didn't.

With the veterinarian's medical knowledge and the support of the entire animal hospital, Kodiak recovered fully. We rejoiced in this animal miracle. Three days later, I returned to my teaching position, knowing that this experience had somehow changed me.

Although everything seemed to be back to normal in my life, internally I was troubled beyond imagination. The ordeal, or "Kodi's accident," as it became known, continued to disturb me. Poodles were bred as German water retrievers and Kodiak, like his ancestors, is a strong swimmer. An expert dog trainer had worked with Kodi to make him "pool safe," so I was secure in his ability to get in and out of the pool. Over time, the gnawing feeling that this accident did not make sense grew stronger.

Three months later everything flew into turmoil when Kodiak had his first seizure. The vet, hoping this was an isolated occurrence, treated the incident conservatively with observation and reassurance. One week later a second seizure struck. I panicked. Remaining calm was an impossibility. Kodiak was placed on a program of phenobarbitol to control future seizures. Reminded that Kodi had conceivably sustained brain damage, I was asked to accept, that in all likelihood, I would never really know what happened the morning of his pool accident, nor what triggered the seizures.

I argued with the doctor, telling him I needed to understand. He responded by telling me that there were some things I would never know. I left the animal hospital that day carrying a bottle of phenobarb in my hand, and in my heart, a stubborn unwillingness to accept the possibility that I would never know what had happened.

As days passed sans seizures, a sense of calm returned. Determined to solve what remained a mystery, I vowed to educate myself each day with one bit of information relevant to the accident. Being open to all possibilities was necessary, since I had no idea what I was looking for. I spent hours on the floor of my local bookstore looking through books for more information and listened intently as people shared their stories of animal rescues. Through it all Kodi and I leaned on each other emotionally and became more connected. Somewhere along the way, the idea of speaking to an animal communicator was mentioned. On first consideration, the concept seemed ludicrous because I come from a medical family of dentists and doctors.

With each passing day, options became scarce. The idea of an animal communicator was beginning to seem less absurd. I made a list of eight pet psychics and began calling them. Feeling uncomfortable after initial inquiries, I selected two animal communicators. Rationalizing that we already had spent a vast amount of money on Kodi made me feel less guilty, but not less ridiculous contacting animal psychics. To make things even less plausible, I realized that all of the communicators consulted over the telephone! My rational, medical orientation questioned how this could be possible.

The first person to whom I spoke wanted every bit of information on the accident laid out, *before* proceeding. This request made me doubtful of her abilities, crushed my hopes, and heightened my skepticism. Yet, in some funny way I was relieved, since the entire idea of talking to a person who would talk to my dog remained preposterous. However, I did come away with two interesting insights. First, I learned about flower essences, and second, I observed Kodi act strangely during my conversation with the first psychic. Although Kodi had been calmly dozing on the bed prior to the phone call, once the consultation began, he fidgeted and did not settle down until I hung up the phone. After my phone conversation with the first pet psychic, I was disappointed and disenchanted. I hugged Kodiak, wondering if my vet might actually be right.

And then came the telephone consultation with Lydia Hiby. After the introductory, "Hi and how are you," Lydia asked if there was any particular reason for my call. Having rehearsed my opening line so as not to give away too much information, I simply stated that my dog experienced a life-altering event and I needed help. Anticipating warm fuzzies or at least genuine sympathy, I was taken aback by her response: "Don't tell me anything." (This comment, I later learned was to avoid clouding Lydia's mind with information she preferred to discover on her own.) My lips were sealed. I spoke only when providing answers to her questions:

* Kodiak is the name of the animal. Kodi is his call name.
* His current age is three years.
* He was fourteen weeks old when we got him.
* His breed is Standard Poodle. I volunteered his color, black. (Because Kodi is a pure bred, she did not need a photograph of him. Usually, she requests a photo of mixed breeds.)
* The date of the life-altering event was February 2, 1994.
* The day of the week was Wednesday and the time was early morning.

There was silence. Lydia said nothing. I said nothing. Kodi opened one eye, raised an eyebrow, and let out a rather peaceful sigh as he snuggled against me, thrilled to be lying on our bed. When the silence was broken after an extremely long pause, what followed was unexpected.

Lydia: "Front left paw."

Bonnie: "Front left paw? What are you talking about?"

Lydia: "Front left paw. Something is wrong with his front left paw."

Bonnie: "I didn't call you about his front left paw. Nothing is wrong with his front left paw. I don't know what you are talking about!"

At this point, I began to feel desperate. Lydia was my last chance. Silently, I tried to calm myself, thinking, *Okay, you are in no worse shape than you were before beginning this insanity. Chalk it up to experience. You have wasted money before. Just go along with her and the consultation will be over soon.* The only problem was my own internal conflict. I had foolishly pinned all my hopes on Lydia Hiby. I wanted answers and expected none. But still I hoped. My thoughts were interrupted when Lydia continued asking questions about the damn front left paw.

Lydia: "Did he hurt it?"
Bonnie: "No."
Lydia: "Did he ever fracture it?"
Bonnie: "No."
Lydia: "Is it bruised or sore?"
Bonnie: "No." (By now my voice reflected my frustration.)
Lydia: "Look, maybe you don't understand, but he keeps showing me his front left paw. Until we figure out what it is he wants us to know, he will not talk to me about anything else. Let's go over this again." And so we did.
Bonnie: "His front left paw has never been broken or sprained, I am certain."
Lydia: "I really want you to think about anything that ever happened to that paw, even if it was from his puppy days." (Suddenly, a light bulb went on for Bonnie!)
Bonnie: "When Kodi was six months old we noticed his dew claw had grown back on his front left paw."
Lydia: "That's it! He says to tell you that the last few times he was groomed they forgot to check the nail and if you look now you will see the nail is very long and it's pushing into his skin."
Bonnie: "Oh my God, it is!"
Lydia: "He says he thinks it would be a good idea to have it written on his card at the groomers to remind them to check."
Bonnie: "Yes, I will and I'll take him in tomorrow to have the nail clipped. In the meantime I will put some cotton under it to take the pressure away."
Lydia: "He feels much better. Now, let's see if he will answer me."

And again there was silence. I anxiously waited for Kodi's response to Lydia's questions. A rush of words and fragmented thoughts followed.

Lydia: "He was throwing an emboli ... dizzy ... confused. His head hurt ... terrible headache. He stumbled. He was out side going to the bathroom. Dizzy ... stumbling ... threw a blood clot. Wait a minute. I am confused. You did say this dog is alive? Is he really there?"

Bonnie: "Yes. He is right here on the bed with me."

Lydia: "I feel him out of his body ... in and out of his body. The next thing he shows me he is looking down on himself. He sees you jumping in ... to a pool? Did he drown? Where did you find him?"

Bonnie: "Yes, he drowned and I found him in our pool."

Lydia: "He has no memory of falling in. He was on the verge of death. He became unconscious. He was coming out of his body. He realized he was in water and tried to hold his breath. Everything was spinning. He saw you jump in and reach him. He knows you saved him."

Bonnie: "I did jump in. He wasn't breathing and I found no heart beat or pulse. I tried mouth to mouth but lost the air. I had to make the air stay in, so I put his tongue back in his mouth, held it closed, and did mouth to nose. How did you know this?"

Lydia explained that by "becoming" Kodiak, she was able to look down and see, *through his eyes*, what happened during this traumatic event.

My goal in talking to an animal communicator was to get answers, so it was time to go for broke. I gave Lydia the date of the first seizure, never mentioning the word seizure, and asking only what happened on that date. She informed me that a seizure occurred, filling in details surrounding the episode, including how the dog felt. Lydia was emphatic that the seizure came from a liver problem, not due to epilepsy. She "nailed" the details of the second seizure, again stating with certainty that these attacks were the result of a liver problem. Lydia assured me there was a natural way to detoxify the liver and insisted that I check and discuss any procedures with my veterinarian before proceeding. It wasn't until much later that I learned that Lydia believed Kodi's liver damage was caused by the toxicity of the chlorine in the pool water.

After the first phone call with Lydia, I asked my vet to run a liver blood panel. The results showed Kodiak's level of bilirubin and SGPT liver enzyme functions to be three times above normal. After diligently weighing both pros and cons, I decided to use homeopathy to treat Kodi. The vet determined the homeopathic regimen was harmless, but he admittedly did not hold much stock in the treatment. Lydia stayed in touch by phone and received updates on Kodiak.

About a month later Lydia called, offering to meet me in person at a local horse stable where she was consulting with a horse group. I wanted this face-to-face meeting for several reasons. First and foremost, I wanted to see what she looked like. Next, I wanted her to look directly into Kodi's eyes in order to tell me how he felt. Lastly, Lydia had volunteered to teach me some energy healing, which could benefit Kodi. The idea of helping Kodi heal was therapeutic for me. Essentially it would require learning the location of the liver acupressure points. The technique was something Lydia insisted on teaching me in person.

On an unseasonably hot 110-degree day we met at a horse stable near Los Angeles. Grateful for this opportunity and aware that the dogs attending were invited guests, I was quite prepared to wait hours for Kodi's name to be called. Observing other consultations was educational and fun, and although I stood back, aware of the client's space and relishing the shade, I watched carefully as Lydia fluctuated between quiet, serious conversation, and light chatting and laughter. Kodi was taking it all in, and often having hiked with horses, he was delighted to again be around their aroma and energy.

Finally our name was called. Kodi, usually reserved upon

first meetings, took one look at Lydia and greeted her like an old friend. We went over his most recent liver panel and discussed the slightly lowered numbers. Lydia showed me where to place my hands on Kodi's liver alarm points and impressed upon me the importance of holding him gently, so he could pull away when he was ready. I left that consultation with a strong belief that it was not a matter of whether or not Kodi would fully recover, but *when*. The numbers on the liver panel continued to go down. Over the next couple of months we stayed in touch by phone. Kodi had charmed one more person who loved him and recognized his specialness.

Three months passed and Lydia surprised us with a call. She had appointments with a horse group near our home and offered to stop by and check on Kodi. By the time her truck pulled up, Kodi was excited with anticipation. Acting as the perfect host, he was permitted to run out and greet her while his side kick scampered along. If I had any remaining doubts about believing in Lydia's ability, they were squelched with what transpired in our conversation that day.

Lydia: "I didn't know you had another dog. Kodi never talked about her. Do you have a daughter?"

Bonnie: "Yes."

Lydia: "Is she away at school?"

Bonnie: "Yes."

Lydia: "This was her dog, but no more. This is daddy's little girl! She is the princess!"

Bonnie: "You never knew we had another dog?"

Lydia: "No. Kodi never told me about her. It wasn't important to him!"

Nailed it again! Brandi was our daughter's eighth-grade graduation gift and she had been in our family for three years before Kodi came along. Our daughter was away at college and Brandi had very much become my husband's little girl. How did she know

*Lydia's first home
visit with Kodiak*

BONNIE S. WEINTRAUB

this? At that point, I didn't care. I just believed her. Kodi, she sensed, felt much stronger, healthier, and energetic.

Nine months after I first spoke to Lydia, Kodi's liver panel tested normal. Apparently, this was quite a feat and the veterinarians rejoiced with us. My personal belief is that a variety of factors enabled Kodiak's liver to heal. The healing combination was homeopathics, energy healing known as Reiki, traditional veterinary medicine, and a change of diet to one including organic vegetables and free-range chicken.

As far as my feeling about animal communicators, I went from a complete skeptic to a true believer, much to the initial dismay of those around me. Kodi is living proof of my sound decision. After communicating with Kodi and completing a body scan, Lydia was convinced that Kodi never had genetic epilepsy and that his only two seizures were caused by a malfunctioning liver. Lydia has seen other dogs whose seizures were related to kidney malfunction. She believes that not all seizures involve the brain and a malfunctioning organ can be the cause, most often the liver or kidney. Lydia trusted that when we successfully detoxified his liver, Kodi would live a normal life. Kodi was on a maintenance dosage of phenobarb suitable for a dog of ten pounds. He weighs slightly over sixty pounds. Our vets agree that

Kodi would have had break-through seizures on this dosage if he had epilepsy. He remains seizure free, and now drug free.

Before Kodi's accident I did not know what synchronicity meant. Lydia has told me that Kodiak is my shaman. She treats him with the respect reserved for a wise Native American healer—one who intuitively heals spiritually and physically. People have told me that Kodi's accident happened for a reason. On certain days that seems more believable than on others. There is no doubt that Lydia has profoundly affected the lives of my entire family.

⌒

Until the writing of this book, I never directly asked Bonnie how she perceived our first consultation. I was curious, wondering whether she got the answers she sought—and how she truly felt. Bonnie responded, "I was shocked by how much you got. I placed all my hopes in you, but was so afraid of being disappointed that I expected nothing. But deep down I trusted because you were my last hope. And somehow I knew that you would come through. I don't know what you call that." "High expectations!" I said laughing aloud. "I'm glad I didn't know that at the time."

There are many different ways people put their lives on the line for a loved animal. In Bonnie's case she placed her whole belief system in scientific knowledge on the line. For the sake of her dog, she was willing to risk her comfort and security in going against the status quo. She was willing to be open to other ways of knowing, even from an animal psychic!

Most animals I talk to tell of feeling love and contentment with their human companion. For humans, there is no way to measure the love a human has for an animal. What seems silly to one person may be serious to another. In the case of Leroy, an English Springer Spaniel, and his owner, Richard, their relationship was primary, and Richard would go to great lengths for his dog's happiness. Richard called for a consultation to basically "check-in"—a common practice among long-time clients. Hearing

Richard's voice was the return of a friend.

Originally, consultations revolved around Richard's girlfriends and how Leroy felt about them. The dog was quite candid when he told me about the new girlfriend who did not allow a dog in her house when Richard spent the night. Leroy was relegated to the car where he waited for morning light and the return of his owner. To Leroy's delight, Richard broke up with this woman and began dating another who owned two Golden Retrievers. Leroy was thrilled to have playmates and be part of a family.

Still, the most important person in Leroy's life was Richard. In turn, Leroy was his sidekick, whether it was going from gig to gig with the band named in the dog's honor, or traveling in Richard's pickup truck as he checked various job sites. Richard was the owner of a plumbing construction business and Leroy was his partner. The well-behaved dog had always been welcomed by the guys, even sharing lunch with them. The first time Leroy was told to wait in the truck he looked hurt, and became depressed. Richard, so closely attuned to Leroy, picked up on these feelings. Unfortunately, the dog thought he had done something wrong and was being punished. However, the reason for waiting in the truck was to prevent Leroy from being physically hurt on a dangerous job site. Once this was explained, Leroy waited patiently until Richard returned to the truck.

The highlight of the year was the wonderful vacations Richard planned for the two of them. Initially, Richard had asked me where Leroy wanted to go and the dog visually communicated pictures of long walks in the woods, cool mountain air, and time together. This event became the annual vacation to Yosemite, treasured by them both.

Years ago, when in-home consultations were the norm, a woman requested my help for her Sheltie mix, Sam. The dog's sudden refusal to go into the backyard confused her. Sam had always run to his playground in the backyard, using the sliding door to enter and exit the house. Now, he was so traumatized by being in the rear yard that he used the front yard to relieve himself. Meredith's intuition told her that something serious had happened. On one particular day, when she returned home from work, she noticed a difference in his behavior. Since that time, Sam seemed fearful and completely avoided the backyard.

When I arrived at her home, Meredith introduced me to Sam, who was hiding under a table. Sam was so reluctant to come outside with us that Meredith needed a leash to pull him out of the house. In the backyard, he lay down flat on the ground and began shaking and trembling. Sitting down next to him, he communicated, *I couldn't help! I couldn't help!* Remaining very quiet, and putting myself in Sam's body, I heard someone yelling from the far corner of the yard, *Help me—help me—help me.* Through pictures, Sam showed me how he ran back and forth at the fence line. He was traumatized hearing the call for help and not knowing what to do. Finally, Sam ran back into his house.

I explained to Meredith that it felt as though Sam heard something happen about a block away. I asked if she had read about an unusual incident in the newspaper. She knew about no such incident but added she would not have known because she had been at work. Then Meredith offered to check with a close friend who was a police officer. In the meantime, I suggested using Rescue Remedy, a Bach Flower Essence, to reassure Sam while we attempted to decipher his message. This option was a welcome relief because the veterinarian had recommended Sam be given Valium. Meredith was adamant against tranquilizing him.

A few days later the answer surfaced with the help of Meredith's police connection. On the day in question a person had been murdered a mere two blocks away from Sam and Meredith's home. Neighbors who had been interviewed, reported hearing someone yell and scream. Sam was devastated, thinking he should have helped. Continued use of flower essence remedies, combined with patience and love, helped to restore Sam's confidence. It took nearly six months before Sam could venture into the backyard again and begin to play. The most recent photograph Meredith sent showed Sam looking pretty relaxed and almost happy.

One of the funniest dog consultations I ever had was with

"Lady Bad Dog." There are times when a problem exists within a multiple pet home. This was the situation when I consulted with a "three-dog" family. All the dogs got along well and the owners truly loved each one, but they had questions about *which* of the dogs was responsible for the chaos within their home. It was not a difficult detective case once I was introduced to the third dog, Lady. Lady had been with them since she was a puppy. The Samoyed mix seemed full of mischief—the twinkle in her eye was an obvious hint. She greeted me as I said aloud, "Hello Lady." She responded, *Lady Bad Dog—that's my name!* She showed me "pictures" of herself knocking garbage cans over, swallowing a balloon, and eating an apple pie! The owners validated all of this behavior. They had solved one mystery themselves. Apparently, neighbors had complained that Lady, adept at scaling the fence, had been a regular but uninvited guest. Of course Lady was always back home before her owners returned, so they couldn't understand what dog the neighbors were talking about. However, when the neighbors produced a photograph of Lady on their porch—the evidence was undisputable!

Dennis the Menace in a white fluffy body, walking on four legs, strutted as she showed me how she climbed up on a chair and then onto the counter, asking Bentley, her Maltese mix family member, to follow. Bentley was encouraged to pull the loaf of bread off the counter and throw a party—and get caught. Lady was the quickest, brightest, most manipulative dog I've seen. Lady, the instigator, was able to get the two other dogs to follow. She was proud of all she accomplished and the owners finally had their answer!

A change in behavior for an animal might indicate an existing problem. While some problems are so subtle that it takes a conscious effort to solve the mystery, others are obvious. When the phone rang, Marge told me I was her last resort. Marge has the unique responsibility of rehabilitating, when necessary, and ultimately placing dogs who have been retired from running the Iditarod. The Iditarod is an annual 1,159-mile race, which stretches from Anchorage to Nome, Alaska. The race was begun in

1973 and commemorates a famous midwinter emergency mission to move medical supplies swiftly to Nome during a diphtheria epidemic in the winter of 1925. The competitors, both men and women, are known as mushers. Only the healthiest dogs are selected to be part of Iditarod dog-sled teams.

The dog in question was Kianna who had been a member of one of the most select sled-dog teams in the world. Marge had adopted her. Sad and frustrated, Marge admitted the dog was suffering from seizures that had become a routine part of her life. The veterinarian prescribed phenobarbitol, but Marge did not think this was the solution. After spending $2,500 on vet bills, Marge was still seeking some relief for Kianna. She followed her gut feeling that told her there was a missing piece to the puzzle.

The first meeting with Marge and Kianna took place in November 1994. It was clear that both the dog and the owner were stressed. Passing visual images back and forth, between my mind and Kianna's, it took only a short time for me to feel a physical problem in my own body. Experiencing pain in the area of my liver, I believed that her liver was affected as well. My suggestion, with the consent of Marge's vet, was to naturally detoxify the liver and change Kianna's diet to one rich in more natural food sources. For two weeks there was steady improvement, and then another seizure.

In a follow-up consultation, I tapped into Kianna, picturing her after the seizure and asking her visually if she drank or ate anything unusual. Suddenly, I tasted pumpkin pie! It had to be coming from her, so I asked Marge if Kianna had eaten any before the seizure. Marge confirmed that Kianna had stolen and eaten half of a pumpkin pie. It dawned on me then that in all likelihood her seizures were food related. This dog had a highly sensitive body and eating something out of the ordinary threw her system off. This entire episode was repeated on another occasion when she devoured a box of animal crackers. Junk food did not agree with her system. Keeping Kianna on a simple diet with no party frills seemed the best solution. Marge continues to check in with me on a regular basis and Kianna continues to do well, except for an occasional problem caused by ingesting "gourmet food."

One of my most memorable dog stories involves one of my childhood heroes—Lassie. A Washington, D.C. television studio was preparing to tape a segment for Broadcast House Live. The assistant producer casually mentioned that Lassie was going to be on the show with me! With Collies in my history and Collies in my blood, largely influenced by Lassie, I was overwhelmed. Following this announcement, I was taken to hair and makeup, where there is always a fun-filled, upbeat atmosphere. Mid-sentence, a hush fell over the room, and most likely the building, when someone whispered, "Lassie's in the building. Lassie's here." You would have thought Liz Taylor had entered the studio!

Excused from hair and makeup, I peeked out the door and witnessed what appeared to be the parting of the sea—people stepped back in awe as Lassie began the long walk down the hallway. Lassie's owner and trainer, Robert Weatherwax, did not seem to notice this phenomenon, which must have been a normal happenstance. At the green room door Lassie looked at me and seemed to acknowledge me. Since he (all Lassies have been males) wasn't on a leash, he sat next to me and held up a paw, doing his famous wave. That's all it took for me to lose my composure and become misty eyed. The trainer seemed irked about the attention I was receiving from Lassie and proceeded to find a dressing room in a rather isolated location.

Taping for the TV show began and as usual I was asked questions about what I did as an animal communicator. Things went well and toward the end of the segment, the host asked if I would remain for the second half of the show with Lassie. "Oh, you've got to be kidding," was my immediate reaction. Lassie was seated in a chair next to me, with Robert behind the host, so he could cue the dog. As we sat there, I began asking Lassie nonverbal questions, which unfortunately distracted him from the trainer. Lassie looked directly at me and and put his paw in my lap. His trainer seemed to be slightly annoyed.

The show host requested I ask Lassie what his most difficult trick had been. Lassie visually responded, *Walking backwards.*

And I verbally interpreted Lassie's response. The host looked over his shoulder, waiting for Robert, as the trainer, to confirm this response. Robert's eyes widened with a startled look, he shrugged his shoulders, and muttered under his breath, "I don't know, ask the dog!" Robert seemed a bit unnerved about the entire experience, but when the segment was over he approached me, shook my hand, and said that the demonstration was pretty neat. He admitted that no one had ever communicated with Lassie the way I did and he never saw Lassie act the way he did with me.

Robert seemed to mellow and volunteered that there had been eight Lassies and each dog had a very special presence. He then asked what Lassie thought about his celebrityhood. I was in heaven, happily reporting that Lassie loved his job and took his fame in stride. Lassie communicated that there were many times he had to put the interests of others in front of his own, when people wanted to hug him or touch him, but he loved traveling, being on stage, and performing. Lassie was a true animal ambassador. The effect one animal can have on a vast number of people is quite amazing, as witnessed by Lassie, who first captured my heart when I was a child.

Many of my clients come to me through referrals. Rarely do referrals come from an animal, but Kodiak actually sent a good friend of his, Sabala, another beautiful black Standard Poodle. Since the dogs play together, Sabala and her owner, Judy, met me at Kodi's house. The reason for the consultation was to ask Sabala if she would mind having one more litter of puppies because Judy wanted to keep one of Sabala's puppies.

When Sabala arrived at Kodi's house, she walked in without Judy, her head held high, and came directly over to me. Never having met me before, she introduced herself the way dogs do— wags, kisses, and happy body language. Sabala's owner, slightly embarrassed, followed a few minutes later, explaining that it was uncommon for shy Sabala to behave so boldly!

We visited for a few minutes, but Sabala, impatient and ready to talk, kept sending me visual images of a magnificent white Standard Poodle. Not knowing who this dog was, I innocently said, "Sabala wants to know what happened to the big white Poodle?" Judy was stunned! The flood gates opened and Judy held a box of tissues as she told me about Iwa, her white standard show bitch, who was put to sleep two years earlier.

Sabala communicated that she was quite willing to have a litter of puppies *for Judy*—and for no other reason. Sabala had originally come from a kennel in England and was brought to America by a well-known breeder and groomer of Standard Poodles. Sabala had been with Judy only two years but felt that Judy was the best life had to offer. Sabala felt it was her job to take care of her loyal owner. Sabala showed me "pictures" of her very busy "mom" and wanted Judy to make more time for the two of them to spend together. Eventually, Sabala whelped a litter of seven puppies—five black and two white. Judy decided to keep the white female. Sabala approved this decision.

The dog in my life who captured my heart and soul was named Hunyak. While at a dog show in Puerto Rico, I approached a woman with two nearly all white, Borzois or Russian Wolfhounds. Never having seen this breed up close, I took the opportunity to satisfy my curiosity and asked many questions. I was enthralled by the breed. As it happened, Beatrice Lydecker knew a reputable breeder in Florida and suggested, if I was truly interested in a show dog, to get a puppy from this breeder.

Not too long after this discussion, Beatrice was in Florida on business, and phoned me from the breeder's home. She offered to fly back with a Borzoi puppy for me. Reality set in, along with slight panic, since I had never owned this breed. I was agreeable as long as it was clearly understood that if things did not work out, the puppy could be returned to the breeder. At this point, Ginger (the second) was my only dog. The thought of having two dogs suddenly sent waves of apprehension through me because I didn't know how to love more than one dog at a time. It is not that I was unwilling, I just didn't know what to do. Covering every possible "what if," since this was to be my first show dog, I reluctantly agreed to meet Beatrice and the puppy at the airport.

As I sat parked at the curb, watching Beatrice come up the

walkway with the puppy, I thought, *He looks miserable!* Certainly the puppy was thinking, *What's happened to me? All these cars, traffic. Who are you?* As soon as the van was loaded, I turned to Beatrice and said, "Send him back. Just look at him. He's upset and confused. He's breaking my heart." However, it was difficult to argue with the explanation that followed. Apparently, the pup whose name was Hunyak, Russian for "rascally boy," was being picked on by the big dogs and according to Beatrice, he probably wouldn't have survived. She also felt that Hunyak was the best dog the woman had bred in ten years. Discussion over. He was staying with me.

Hunyak tried to tell me he needed attention and although I tried, I misinterpreted some of the things he did. He seemed unhappy and having a dog that was not totally content, upset me. I was used to Collies who were open and easy to read. Hunyak was a challenge. It wasn't until Ginger became ill and her health declined that I allowed myself to emotionally lean on Hunyak. Until then, my loyalty went to Ginger and she was the number one dog. However, Ginger was thrilled to have a buddy and accepted Hunyak long before I did.

When Ginger died, I finally latched onto Hunyak and began to treasure who he truly was. I affectionately anointed him with the nickname "Bud" and he went everywhere with me. It was during this time that I began to enter Hunyak in dog shows. He seemed to thoroughly enjoy the experience of the dog show circuit and we continued to bond.

As a sight hound, Hunyak was bred to go after game, however, he had a very gentle nature. Borzois' temperament and personality reflect the fact that they were first bred for aristocracy. Both regal and elegant, their job was to chase packs of wolves for kings. Hunyak was a perfect specimen. He came alive in the show ring. Hunyak had so much to offer the breed and I was thrilled to show him. Once he had his championship, a new dream was fulfilled when I took him to the Westminster Dog Show in Madison Square Garden. This dream was realized twice. Although Hunyak never won his class, both times he made the final cut, recognized for his specialness. Those memories I will treasure forever.

In the early 1990s my mother was diagnosed with cancer and slowly her health deteriorated. Since we were separated by 3,000 miles, I offered to move east for several months at a time to care for her. At one point I told my mom that I could not visit her without bringing Hunyak. Her reaction was predictable, "Do you really need him? Never mind, I know the answer to that question. Bring him. Just bring him." As it turned out, everyone benefited from Hunyak's company. Nurses, priests, family, and anyone else coming through the door were greeted by Hunyak with his human-like graciousness. My mother never thought she could love another dog after her Ginger, but Hunyak found a way to her heart. He sensed when to go into her room and put his head on her bed. In turn, she thanked him with dog cookies and a kiss. Hunyak gave me the emotional support I needed while I cared for my dying mother.

After my mother died and I was adjusting to the loss, I decided to get another dog. Ginger had passed on and I wanted another Collie. I wrestled with the idea because of the closeness Hunyak and I shared. But I also knew that he needed to play with a dog buddy. After researching breeders and visiting different litters, I decided on a lovely female Collie whom I named Petals. She became Hunyak's buddy and she brought him exuberant joy. Even as other dogs continued to join the family, Hunyak always protected Petals and instructed other dogs to treat her with care.

All seemed right with the world. Then, on a lovely spring weekend, while working at a family pet show, I received an emergency phone call from my secretary. Hunyak had broken his leg and because it was evening, he was being taken to the emergency clinic. My mind raced as the car seemed to drive itself. I was grateful to be living in a time when emergency clinics are available to help when the traditional veterinary hospitals close for the night. Hunyak was splinted and because the break was diagonal with a bone fragment, plans were made to

LYDIA HIBY

Hunyak and Petals

have him see his regular vet the following morning.

Because the break was serious, bone surgery was necessary. The surgery involved inserting a pin and wrapping wire around the bones. It was determined that this technique would give him the best chance for recovery. The hope was to stabilize the break and ultimately allow the leg to heal.

Hunyak emerged from the surgery wearing his first cast of many. His recovery was followed carefully with office visits and a succession of x-rays. After two months, an ominous grayish shadow appeared on the x-ray. The radiologist broke the news that Hunyak had bone cancer. When my emotional numbness subsided, serious decisions were staring me in the face.

Deciding against chemotherapy was relatively simple, having watched my mom endure the treatment. I opted against removing Hunyak's leg because he was not a young dog at ten-and-a-half years old. It was his rear leg, and although many dogs do well as tripods, this was not right for him. The remaining choice was homeopathic treatment and that became the method we followed. Calling everyone I knew, and drawing from vast sources of knowledge, Hunyak was ultimately placed on a program that consisted of twenty-one supplements. His coat was fabulous. His appetite was hearty. The California weather that winter was warm and wonderful, filled with sparkling sunny eighty-degree days. It was difficult to comprehend that Hunyak, who looked wonderful, was still fighting cancer.

I had always promised Hunyak a yard of his own because the two houses we had lived in previously had little postage stamp yards, with no lush grass to run through. When we moved to our new home, I announced that the front yard was his. Hunyak even dug himself a little dirt scoop declaring it his turf. He enjoyed his yard and cherished the people who always stopped by to visit with him at the fence. The big cast never hindered his fluid movement as he happily patrolled his yard.

In mid-January, his energy began to fade. As Hunyak's physical being began to weaken, I second guessed the information I was receiving from him. I started to depend on close friends to validate what I believed to be Hunyak's messages. I worried that I might miss a message—not hear him ask to be released from his body and be set free. It is very difficult to communicate with your own animal, one who is ill and might be in pain. As his mother, I wanted only to make the cancer go away. Many times I thought about the uncanny similarities between Hunyak and my mother battling cancer. Without being overbearing, I continued to check in with Hunyak often. I implored him to tell me when he was ready to be released from his body. Some days his messages were clear, *I'm having a hard day today.* Other times, *This cast doesn't bother me at all—look at me go!* But always, Hunyak would tell me, *Thank you for letting me keep my leg.* He said that keeping his leg enabled him to maintain his dignity.

After two very difficult days, I slept with Hunyak on the floor knowing it would be our last night together. With the help of a veterinarian, Hunyak was put to sleep in his home, surrounded by the two other people who loved him the most, my roommate and my secretary. I whispered to Hunyak that he could be with his grandma, my mom, who had adored him. As soon as Hunyak's breathing stopped, the three of us looked at each other and then simultaneously looked out the window. Hunyak was flying around in his front yard, running as fast as he could. He was doing what he loved to do. In a blink, Hunyak's spirit vanished, having said his last good-bye.

Lydia with Hallie and Rusty

CARL HIBY

Chapter Four

CAT MUSINGS

Oh cat; I'd say, or pray: be-ooootiful cat!
Delicious cat! Exquisite cat! Satiny cat! Cat like
a soft owl, cat with paws like moths, jewelled
cat, miraculous cat! Cat, cat, cat, cat.

— DORIS LESSING

A s in any species, every cat is an individual. There will be those who are loving and nurturing and others who are reserved and aloof. Cats own the reputation of remaining distant physically and emotionally. Often thought to be unapproachable, I believe the cat is simply misunderstood. We expect dogs to be loyal, and to love unconditionally. However, the relationship between a cat and a human is entirely different. Generally, we expect a cat to be a cat. And we happily accept felines in all their manifestations.

There is a magnet hanging on my refrigerator that reads, "Cats are not like dogs. If you call a cat you can leave a message and they may get back to you." A cat will do what he wants, when he wants, where he wants, and with whom he wants. A person capable of overpowering a small animal, can hold a cat, but if the cat does not want to be held, he will somehow break away from the constraint. Cat owners accept, and admire the cat's independence.

The grandest honor bestowed upon a human is when the cat *chooses* to come to those arms on her own. The strongest statement of affection in its truest and most pure form is the sound of a deep, slow purr. Nothing can replace or substitute the sound of the *brrrrrrrr*—the natural motor emanating from the cat's soul.

Admittedly, until age twenty-two, when my first cat *allowed* me to enter her life, I was a stranger to the cat world. It takes a special kind of person to appreciate a feline, and clients who own cats seem to share certain traits. Regardless of gender, cat owners are among the most sensitive people I have worked with and they are unique—perhaps like the cat! Many of my cat clients meditate and perceive the cat to be a spiritual animal. For me, my enlightenment of felines began with my first cat, Jane, but it was the experience of working at The Cat Practice in New York's Greenwich Village that opened my eyes to the cat's universe.

Trusting that everything happens for a reason, the circumstances that led me to The Cat Practice confirm this belief. The Cat Practice had obtained background information about me through the vet tech registry and wanted to interview me for a job. Fate, along with some prodding from my mother, pushed me toward the interview even though at the time I had no affinity for cats. Until entering this feline-only clinic, my experience was limited to cats I had worked with in traditional animal hospitals. Typically, cats in traumatic situations are all claws and resemble a Tasmanian devil. Considering myself a devout dog person, I had no desire to get to know cats.

The head veterinarian at The Cat Clinic, Dr. Skip Sullivan, surprised me during the job interview by querying, "You don't look very comfortable about this—do you have a problem with cats?" I remember uttering, "Not really," and going on to explain that whenever I had opened a cat's cage door at an animal clinic, the feline made a growling sound at me. Then I became brutally honest and stated that being in a pit with dogs was preferable to hearing that cat noise. "Besides, I have no idea how to deal with cats," I admitted. "I never had one as a child."

The vet listened carefully, and then explained his dilemma. At the moment he was without a technician and he had ten surgeries scheduled for the following day. He was in a predicament and his request was close to a plea. He offered to pay me for the day, and if I did not like it, I could leave with no hard feelings. I agreed. Dr. Sullivan introduced me to the staff; Virginia, the receptionist and Barney, the recovery nurse. That was it. Just the vet and the two employees—and the missing vet tech. It was an intimate facility.

The Cat Practice was an unconventional place, located on a third floor loft. Everything was wooden. There was no stainless steel furniture and nothing in the clinic felt cold or foreboding. Dr. Sullivan purchased the practice from another vet, a husband and wife team, who implemented some unique ideas. They were convinced that cats do better on wood—even the surgery table was wood treated with a sealant. Instead of cages for the cats there were wooden nooks, which looked like sections in an armoire. These spaces reminded me of the wooden compartments used to stock men's shirts in a fine clothing store. One section of nooks was reserved for contagious animals who needed to be quarantined. A glass panel served as the front of the nook and each nook was equipped with its own independent air-filtration system. Quiet fans continually circulated the air. I was impressed by the thoughtful care given to the cats and the creation of an environment so comfortable and safe.

That first day, as we worked together, Dr. Sullivan explained that his philosophies paralleled those of the founding veterinarians. His fundamental beliefs included gentle handling of all cats, refusal to declaw any feline, and the reward of catnip following every examination. Personalized attention was given to each cat after surgery. Post-surgery, as the anesthetic wears off, I observed each cat gently waking up in the recovery nurse's lap. She would stroke the cat and whisper words of comfort.

That one day of work turned into three years. It was at this astounding clinic with its intimate setting and its charming wood and wicker furnishings, that I became a cat person and learned how to deal with these special animals. It was easy to keep an open mind as I constantly learned from Dr. Sullivan and discovered new and more effective methods for treating these sensitive animals. Each decision was made with thoughtful concern regarding what was best and most comfortable for the cat. From the beginning, I was exposed to many bits of wisdom, often in direct conflict with what I had observed in traditional clinic settings.

For example, The Cat Practice used catnip as a pre-anesthetic. Catnip is an herb. Usually number one on the list of a cat's most favorite things, catnip gives the animal a temporary high but it is not addictive. Cats eat it, roll in it, and snort it. I had heard catnip called "Cosmic Catnip," but when "kitty cocaine" was mentioned, it made me wonder if I had heard correctly. I had. At The Cat Practice the vet gave catnip to every cat awaiting surgery because it helped the animal relax and therefore less anesthetic was required. Afterwards, the cat woke up nicely and gently in a comforting human lap.

I grew to respect the cats' sensitivities and their acrobatic talents. How many animals can invert themselves totally? And how many do you know who can sit and groom their stomachs? No longer did I consider myself solely a dog person. It was around this time that I took my first animal communication class. With the techniques I learned and the continual information gained from working at The Cat Practice, my confidence grew steadily. Interacting with cats became quite matter of fact.

Many cats have touched me with their stories. Renfield was one of those special cats. A huge orange cat with a full white ruff, Renfield had been left at The Cat Practice by an owner who decided to leave the cat rather than pay his vet bill. Renfield became our house cat, and was loved by all. Over a couple of weeks I noticed a subtle increase in the amount of water Renfield consumed and thought he was not feeling well. Dr. Sullivan ran a blood panel with negative results. For some reason, I kept thinking Renfield was diabetic, although I had never known a diabetic cat and had only heard about one such case. Although my animal communication skills were still underdeveloped, I was drawn to Renfield and continued observing him. Without realizing that my intuition was the nagging feeling that persisted, I spoke to Dr. Sullivan again. He ran a glucose test and sure enough, Renfield was diabetic. My knowledge about the disease was infinitesimal but I soon became somewhat of an expert.

Every morning we had to get a urine sample from Renfield in order to regulate his insulin. You can imagine how hard that was. We came up with the idea of filling a cat pan with shredded newspaper and securing it on a slight tilt. The only way Renfield would get his breakfast was if he "held it" until I got to the clinic. He would hear me walking up to the third floor and he would peek out the window making certain the footsteps were mine. He would spot me and wail, *Hurry up and get up here. I'm waiting to pee!* Once I put the key in the door Renfield would go flying into his bathroom, and leave a urine specimen in the metal cat pan. Then I would check the insulin level with a dipstick, give Renfield his injection, and finally, breakfast. He was a happy cat, and smart too. It took him only two days, until he understood precisely what he had to do. Renfield made the connection that breakfast was withheld until he produced a urine sample. He knew exactly what was going on. Although I may have unknowingly communicated with Renfield, simply by envisioning the procedure that was necessary to keep him alive, I never sat down with him and verbally explained the details. I defer to Renfield and give this cat full credit for figuring out the necessary steps.

Because Renfield was monitored in an animal hospital we were successful in controlling his illness. But diabetes is difficult to control in a cat and although it can be done, it entails a huge commitment. Since we had a lab available it was simple to take a tiny pipette, prick the tip of his ear and check his blood value whenever necessary. Renfield lived a long and full life even though most diabetic cats do not.

The majority of our cat patients were ordinary house cats. We did see some celebrity show cats but a significant percentage of the clientele was the typical, much loved family pet. During a routine day, a rather flustered woman showed up at The Cat Practice carrying a cat she rescued from a dumpster. She was a restaurant owner and had gone to the dumpster in the back alley and noticed the cat licking out of a can. The cat was bleeding from his mouth, so she wrapped him up and sought help. The cat's tongue was cut in half. The woman offered to pay for the cat to be euthanized, but Dr. Sullivan, a devoted humanitarian, asked for a couple of days, hoping the tongue might heal itself. Although a scar was visible, the tongue actually fused together. In celebration of his determination to live, we gave him a name—Tigger.

Unfortunately, Tigger was left with handicaps. He drooled because the side of his mouth had been injured, and he had trouble swallowing and needed to be hand fed. He taught me a great deal about patience and compassion. I had never spent time around a feral cat, and it took time and effort to establish trust. Eventually, a small access room with a rocking chair became his castle. At first, when I entered, all the hairs on his body would stand up. He growled, announcing that he was ready to take me on. Slowly, we got to know each other and he would climb into my lap as I rocked in the old chair. He remained in our makeshift rehabilitation center until five months later when we found the special home he needed. Tigger's teachings are still with me. Through his wisdom, I developed more empathy, felt his pain, and became sensitive to an emotionally debilitated and physically handicapped animal.

The empathy I learned at The Cat Practice helps me in my work today as an animal communicator. A few years ago, I had a consultation with a couple to discuss the health of their cat, Tyrone, an American short hair, silver classic tabby. Tyrone was plagued with sinusitis. My recommendation was that Tyrone be treated with acupuncture. Months later I received a follow-up letter saying that Tyrone was doing well. One of the owners, Glenn, wrote to me about his special relationship and the effect of his consultation with me as an animal communicator.

Tyrone is my cat and I am his human. We share time in the backyard as he sniffs the air, chases butterflies, munches a succulent grasshopper, or catches an occasional mouse, or even a gopher or two. During our quiet time he looks into my eyes and I look into his. I am his guardian and he reassures me from the hard knocks of life with a tender and enchanting purr.

You told me things about Tyrone's relationship with the other cats in my care. A stray named Zeke—who needed a home. Dimitrie's jealousy. You mesmerized me. It was like Tyrone was speaking to me. We communicate, but this was different. I learned about his headaches, his good days and bad. You made me feel closer, more connected to him. It was a wonderful experience, one I will always remember.

– Glenn

I am grateful that clients take the time to send notes and keep information current concerning the status of their pets. It is always interesting to learn how my suggestions have been implemented, especially since some of my suggestions may seem unconventional or mysterious to the pet owner. One unusual situation happened with Carolyn who called me even though she was skeptical about my abilities as an animal communicator. A breeder of Abyssinian cats, she had several cats who lived in the house. For some reason, unbeknownst to Carolyn, one female cat, Jedda, was constantly involved in battle. When the combat became intense, she asked me to speak to Jedda.

The cat explained that she was so petrified of the other cats attacking her that she protected herself by attacking first. My suggestion was to buy Jedda something that would make her feel special. Perhaps she might respond well to the idea of a "power collar." I told Jedda she was a good cat and a special cat, and when she wore the "power collar" none of the other cats would torment her. I envisioned the collar making Jedda feel safe and confident. Jedda showed me a collar that she would like by picturing a flashy, shiny bejeweled collar. I passed this information on to Carolyn, who went shopping and returned with a collar bedecked with rhinestones. The moment Carolyn put the collar around Jedda's neck the fighting ceased! After that success story, Carolyn went from skeptic to believer.

Another success story using positive reinforcement also took place with Carolyn, who was concerned about Talkalot, otherwise known as "Talkie." Although the cat earned a grand championship, Talkie's disdain of cat shows was evident, much to Carolyn's dismay. The cat became difficult and obnoxious as soon as she was around a show atmosphere. One weekend Carolyn was asked to collect tickets at the entrance of a local cat show. For no other reason besides wanting Talkie's company, Carolyn decided to take the cat with her. The day of the show, Talkie sat patiently on the entrance table and seemed quite pleased by all the positive attention she received. When the cat decided it was time to get down and go for a stroll, quick-thinking Carolyn tied a purple helium balloon with a long string to Talkie's harness. This way the cat could easily be spotted as she walked about the show. Carolyn was stunned by this sudden change in Talkie's attitude. In a consultation later, Talkie told me she now loved cat shows and was content with her self-appointed role of spokescat. Talkie was thrilled with the recognition the purple balloon attracted and she enjoyed standing apart from the other cats. It was not the cat show itself that Talkie disliked, but rather the procedure of being shown.

Most times when I make recommendations to help an animal with a behavioral change, I advocate positive reinforcement. I have yet to meet an animal that will not respond to praise. When the owners understand what the animals need, then owners and animals can work in unison to accomplish acceptable behaviors. The scratching post is a wonderful example. Cats have an intrinsic desire to scratch. The reason cats act out this particular behavior is two fold: First, the need to put their scent or identity on an object, and second, to trim their nails. (The desire is not to destroy furniture or draperies!) Cats seek out surfaces that are nubby, or they search for something that can shred, like wicker. But if the owner provides a scratching post that suits a cat's need, the furnishings will be left intact.

Unfortunately, many store-bought posts are aesthetically pleasing to the owner rather than to the cat. If the carpet nap is too long, the cat is apt to get hung up in the long fibers and will likely reject the post. More pleasing to a cat is sisal or carpet wrapped around a log with the jute backing exposed. Cats must get attention each time they use a scratching post. Positive reinforcement is necessary for success. (Send a mental picture of your cat using the scratching post.) Even if I am on the phone, I will stop for a moment and praise my cats for using the scratching post. Sometimes I put catnip on their post. Most important, the scratching post must be centrally located. You would not put a child's playpen in an isolated area and expect a contented baby, would you? Also speak to your cat and tell him or her, "Respect my furniture by using your furniture."

I advocate treating all animals in the most natural way and it is only as a last resort that I break from my norm. Extreme measures are necessary if a cat, because of destroying furniture, is in jeopardy of losing its home. When an owner is contemplating taking the cat to the pound, I recommend as a last resort truth or consequences, "You must use your scratching post or you will get declawed." In my opinion, declawing a cat is more humane than turning a cat over to a shelter to be euthanized. The reality is that having a cat declawed and remaining in its home outweighs the prospect of being left at the pound.

The College for Cats has a series of classes for owners and their felines who are preparing to work in front of a camera. Classes include a "costume tolerance test," where the cat's comfort level is judged. Sandi Wirth, the founder, believes in positive reinforcement, compliments, and expressions of approval to entice her cats to try their hardest.

One of Sandi's rescued cats, Mannix, first brought us together. A black long-haired cat, Mannix came with a very loud, threatening hiss. Instead of teaching him to stop hissing, Sandi praised the sound and complimented the cat on his "good hiss." The outcome was a "hiss" on demand! Mannix and his famous hiss have appeared in numerous television shows and movies. When Sandi called me, Mannix was ill. After speaking to Mannix, I sensed kidney and stomach problems. I suggested Sandi treat the physical problems with natural remedies with her vet's approval. The condition was temporary and once Mannix recuperated, he returned to work.

So often a cat's problems are easily solved. Incorrect diet can cause difficulty, even if the food is of the highest quality. For example, it is a fact that most cats love fish, but only the Russian Fishing Cat requires fish in its diet. Fish is unnatural to a cat's diet and too much fish may result in a condition known as steatitis, an overabundance of vitamin E. However, cats are carnivores and they do require meat in their diets, but there needs to be a balance.

More than any other problem, cat owners consult me about litter box problems. "Out of potty experiences," a term that originally appeared in a cat magazine, is what I use to categorize these situations. Cats are very particular, and because each cat has specific preferences, I will ask a cat many questions before offering a solution to each cat box problem.

In the wild, a cat urinates in water because the odor is offensive. A domestic cat may find the scent so disagreeable he or she does not want to share a litter box with the other household cats. Some cats want odorless litter. Some want shredded newspaper. Oftentimes, cats brought up on shredded newspaper do not know how to use litter. Some felines want a covered cat box, while others want it uncovered. Occasionally, one cat may feel so intimidated and fearful that another cat will pounce, the cat is unable to walk to the litter box. The number of preferences a cat has concerning litter box issues are as vast as the varied reasons a horse will not get into a trailer.

Myrna called about her black cat, Boo, who had begun using the bath mat in front of his cat box, rather than his cat box. She was frustrated and wanted my help. I explained to her that cats will put their own smell (by urinating) on something that smells offensive to them. In Boo's situation the bath mat was new and to him the rubber backing had a foul smell. Interestingly, rubber-backed bath mats are the number-one culprits with litter box problems. In addition, cats seem to find plastic shopping bags and any clothes or bedding dried with fabric softener sheets equally offensive. Boo told me, *I liked my new uncovered cat box.* He also communicated,

I liked my old litter because it did not give me a headache. Myrna was quite surprised, explaining that she recently had switched to a scented litter thinking it might help. Scented litters often bother a cat by causing headaches. My recommendation was to remove the bath mat and get rid of the scented litter. Two weeks later, Myrna called with a follow-up report. The problem was solved!

When I am attempting to solve a problem with a cat, it is not uncommon to ask many questions. Thomas is my special kitty, the most surreptitious of all. Of course, all of my cats are special, but Thomas must have been sent to me because I still can't figure out where he came from! My Collie, Ginger, and I were walking under a freeway overpass late one Sunday evening. It was unusually quiet, there was no traffic and we were very much alone—just us and the stillness. I turned and looked over my shoulder in response to a meow, and "poof," a tiny kitten stood where seconds before was nothing. The Russian Blue kitten could not have been more than six-weeks old and likely was the runt of the litter. He obviously had been taken away from his mother too soon because he nursed on my sweater as I held him.

Thomas remained in isolation at the clinic where I worked until he grew stronger and was given a clean bill of health. I put the word out that the little guy was available for adoption. A woman wanting a Russian Blue chose Thomas and he left to begin his life of luxury; however, their life together was short lived because she returned him to the clinic twenty four hours later. Thomas, it seems, nursed on any fabric he could find and her sweatshirt was covered with wet spots. Because I found Thomas and felt responsible, I took him home. He joined the family and grew up only resorting to suckling when he was severely stressed.

Thomas grew strong and confident and became a proficient bully. Even my belief in positive reinforcement seemed hopeless with Thomas. I resorted to all the methods I detest—I yelled at him, threatened him, and even misted him with a spray bottle. Thomas could have cared less. He chased the other cats, tormented them, and enjoyed every minute. At this time he was a "rebellious teenager," and I was inexperienced in disciplining cats.

Beatrice Lydecker had a solution—kitty jail. I was instructed to take an open mesh plastic milk crate, turn it upside down, and place it in the middle of our living room floor. The next time Thomas displayed his rude behavior, I was to stop him, correct him, and tell him that if he chased another cat he was going to "kitty jail." It took only minutes until the opportunity arose and I did exactly as instructed. Thomas stopped chasing Missy long enough to give me a funny look as I offered the ultimatum.

Several minutes passed before he repeated his unacceptable action. This time I picked Thomas up, told him he was going to kitty jail because he chased Missy, and placed him within the overturned milk crate in the middle of the room. Within minutes all the cats, even the most timid, came out of hiding to look at Thomas. Obviously, Thomas was embarrassed. Ten minutes later Thomas was released from jail, and he only repeated his offense two more times until he figured out what he was not allowed to do. Years later, if Thomas even started to pick up speed as if to chase, I reminded him about "kitty jail," and he would immediately put on the brakes.

If you decide to try this, make sure the jail time is short. For obvious reasons, do not use a carrying crate that is also used for the visits to the vet. It would be unwise to punish the cat in the enclosure you want the cat to think of as her sanctuary. Use a plastic milk-type crate that can be seen through. Place the jail in a central part of your home so the guilty party is not isolated, but embarrassed. Explain to your cat by first warning her what will happen.

⌒

Cats fascinate me because they are the near perfect or "original" animal. The appearance of many animals has evolved over time, but since cats have been on earth, they have remained virtually unchanged except for minor variations of the ears and the tail. There have been no physical or structural changes to the cat's body. Very few creatures besides the cat, the snake, and the shark have remained untouched through evolution. Yes, we have made cats cobby and developed longer hair coats but the cat's basic skeletal structure has not changed.

Unfortunately, there are many remaining myths that surround cats, among them how much cats hate water. I had a client who wanted to know which of her three cats was flushing the toilet all day while she was at work because her water bill was three times what it should have been. After a consultation with the cat, I found out that yes, indeed, one of her cats spent the day playing with the toilet handle as she watched the water swirl down the toilet. Another client had cat company every evening when drawing a bath. The cat joined in and swam laps in the tub! When I questioned, *Why*, the cat replied, *It was fun!*

Most everyone has heard the myth that cats smother babies. I hope Nancy's story will put that idea to rest. Nancy first called me when she and her husband were preparing for the birth of their first child. When they had married two years earlier, her husband came with Snowball, his fifteen-year old cat. Nancy's concerns focused around introducing Snowball to the infant, once the baby arrived. I communicated long distance with Snowball and discovered that he was very excited to have a new person in the family. He liked Nancy from their first meeting and she was the first female to whom he felt connected.

However, the follow-up phone call stunned me. One night, two weeks after coming home with the baby, Nancy had finished nursing her son and put him in his crib. Exhausted, the new mother fell into a deep sleep only to be awakened by the cat sitting on her chest, swatting her nose as if to say, *Wake up, wake up*. Still groggy, Nancy pushed Snowball away. The cat persisted. This time she sat up, taking notice of the wild look in his eyes. Before her feet hit the floor, Snowball dashed into the nursery. Nancy followed and panicked as she watched the animal leap into the crib. The baby was gasping for breath, suffocating in the crib blankets. Nancy reacted by tossing the cat out of the crib. Then she grabbed the infant who had begun to turn blue. The baby's life was saved. After that Snowball slept with the child every night, first in his crib and then on his bed. In every baby picture, beside the adored son, sat the adored cat. Snowball lived until age twenty and the two boys spent five wonderful years together.

I was faced with an unusual situation that involved a cat and children. When I got a call for help from Deena, she was concerned about her ten-and-one-half year old, brown-and-white patch, tabby, Nakeeta. Deena runs a daycare program for children in her Northern California home.

Deena had adopted Nakeeta from a neighborhood family that had been rough with the cat. Nakeeta fit into Deena's life and the transition was smooth. After the rough handling Nakeeta received from the original family, Deena thought it ironic that the cat was still drawn to the children at the daycare center. The cat plopped himself down in the middle of the circle when story time began, paying close attention to the plot—never taking his eyes off his new "mom."

Deena explained that Nakeeta had reached out to a new boy, Kyle. Kyle had never been around cats and was at first afraid of Nakeeta. But little by little, day by day, Nakeeta edged closer to the boy—until finally they shared nap time together on the same blanket. Nakeeta ended up resting on Kyle's chest and a powerful bond developed between them.

Then Kyle was absent for two days. Deena became concerned and Nakeeta became depressed. The cat developed respiratory symptoms even though his inoculations were current, and he was strictly an indoor cat. It was during this time that Deena had called me, concerned about Nakeeta's illness. Nakeeta "showed me" how he joined the kids on the floor at nap time, and in particular laying on Kyle's blanket with him. When I asked Nakeeta to explain what happened, he said, *I'm trying to take the boy's illness away.* When Kyle regained his health and returned to the play group, Nakeeta's health rebounded.

In 1990 Morris, a ten-year old cat, was brought into the animal hospital by his owner, Carol. This large, long-haired cat had been mauled by two dogs. Major surgery was required to close gaping stomach wounds and the cat fought for life. Carol checked to see if Morris survived and then she disappeared, never returning to pick up Morris or pay her bill. She assumed we would continue to care for Morris. However, by not returning to the hospital, Carol did not take responsibility for making the ultimate choice about his future.

If a cat is left at an animal hospital under these circumstances it is common for the cat to be put up for adoption or euthanized. I communicated with Morris and determined that he felt abandoned and that he was resigned to dying. Morris was uncertain whether or not he could handle living with anyone else. I felt so strongly that since this cat fought to survive, and won the battle, he deserved to live. I decided to take him to join my family of cats and dogs. Despite his past history of being mauled by canines, Morris said, *I am not afraid of your dogs.* Morris never had a problem getting along with any of my dogs nor did any one of them ever give Morris a difficult time. In fact Morris became so confident that he strutted around "his" house, demanding respect and getting it. He even purposely blocked doorways. Because of his injuries, he lay down on his side, looking like a ripe pumpkin, declaring, *I'm not moving. You go around me.* The other animals listened and acknowledged Morris as the ruler until he died five years later at the age of fifteen.

Frequently before finding me, a client has gone round in circles trying to find a solution to a problem. Liza and her tabby, Francie, had gone through a difficult two-year period of medical disillusionment. Liza was eventually referred to me through a pet store that specializes in natural products, but her story really begins when she volunteered at an animal shelter.

Liza's love of animals propelled her to Pet Orphans, a humane animal rescue organization. Shelter work is emotionally draining, but Liza was able to remain detached from the animals they rescued—that is, until she met Francie. Francie's arrival at the shelter was unusual, even by shelter standards. Francie was carried into Pet Orphans by a kind soul who found her in church with an attached note that read:

I am a loving but feisty little girl. Please help me.

Liza was drawn to this wonderful spirit who was named in honor of St. Francis of Assisi. However, Francie suffered from a chronic skin condition. Liza was determined to help Francie heal and restore the feline's coat to health. Francie had patches of missing fur and looked moth eaten. In spite of the cat's appearance, Liza adopted Francie, *knowing* she could help. The road to finding a healthy solution was hardly what Liza anticipated. After nine months, holistic methods proved disappointing. The next attempt was traditional medicine, which included a full year of antibiotics and cortisone treatment. This did not solve the problem either. Frustrated, Liza visited a natural pet shop for some remedies and was given my name.

I spoke to Francie and took her back in time, asking her what life was like before she was carried into Pet Orphans. *I'm a gentle man's cat*, she replied. Francie then pictured walking around in "dad's" garage, and added, *I'm with dad all the time. I'm with him when he works*. Francie "showed me" that her dad did welding and metal work in the garage, and I watched Francie walk through the residue, the powder left from the metal shavings. Additionally, I sensed the pungent smell of shellac. These factors were the connection, I believed, that caused the chronic skin condition.

Francie told me, *I used to be pretty*, and although she does not see herself as ugly, the cat very much wants her lush coat returned. Francie was exhausted from the months of medical treatment, and with conviction she declared, *I am tired of living under a microscope*. (Once I have talked to an animal and picked up its pictures and feelings, I then put these fragments into a dialogue so the owner can understand what the animal is communicating. It was the feeling of being stared at by doctors— poked and prodded that led me to use the word, "microscope" in my interpretation of this conversation.)

My suggestions were for a treatment program that incorporated flower essences and a natural detoxification process. Also, a change in diet to include fresh organ meat, such as liver. And I suggested using crystals in the cat's water dish to provide healing energy. Liza is working with a medical group who shares this philosophy and has been told patience is a necessity. Natural healing cannot be rushed.

Liza updates me regularly. Francie continues to work with the natural detoxification program and recently it was discovered that Francie is highly reactive to diatomaceous earth, which is the base powder in flea powder products. Chiropractic adjustments have been added to aid in Francie's recovery. Liza says Francie has more interest in life and has just begun to groom herself, stretch, and use her scratching post—very favorable signs. Most promising is that Liza notices Francie's increased interest in daily life and a general contentment.

Lydia Hiby during a consultation

Chapter Five

THE
VELVET TOUCH

And God took a handful of southerly wind, blew
his breath over it and created the horse.

– BEDOUIN LEGEND

There is a magical coexistence between a horse and a human. For those of us who are horse lovers we realize how all consuming this passion can be. Once you have gazed into a horse's big expressive eyes, and had his warm breath gently caress your face, the yearning for the velvet touch changes your life forever. For me, there was a special horse who would rekindle my childhood passion for horses.

Weekend consultations, primarily with horse groups, take me all over the United States. Traveling has become second nature to me—packing and unpacking a way of life. In February 1995, I spent a weekend communicating with horses at a barn in Nebraska. As expected, I found a wide range of personalities among them, for each horse has a distinct identity. It was a cold Nebraska winter, and I couldn't seem to get warm as I walked through the barn. But when I spotted a horse who was standing in the corner of his stall, with his head hanging down, I momentarily forgot the cold. For whatever reason, I was drawn to this tall, dark, and handsome gelding. His name was Winter Chocolate since he was darker than the finest bittersweet.

I easily picked up on Winter Chocolate's feelings of being lonely, sad, and very disillusioned with life. His owner did not book a consultation with me, but I did learn from others at the barn that his owner provided physical care—food, shelter, and medical—but did not satisfy Winter Chocolate's emotional hunger. There were no hugs, carrots, trail rides, or kisses meant to be placed on this horse's velvet nose. Each time Chocolate popped into my consciousness, I thought back to my childhood, and the pony rides, and the horses I had cared for and loved—and the kisses I left on their velvet noses.

When I returned to California, the memory of Chocolate with his dark haunting eyes and his soulfulness did not fade away. I stayed in touch with the barn manager in Nebraska, always asking about Chocolate, and sadly learned that his owner rarely came to visit. He had no bad habits that I could detect, so it made no sense to me that such a loving animal should stand in a pasture day after day—month after month, season after season—with relatively no human contact. I wondered why someone would own a horse and not spend time with the animal.

When I heard Chocolate was for sale, I immediately bought him, and had him shipped to his new home in California. Later, I learned that Chocolate was originally from California and had only moved to Nebraska four years prior—so he really was returning home. In essence, I had adopted a 1,500-pound baby that stood seventeen-hands high. He had to learn many things, but most important, he needed to learn to trust me. When I told Chocolate something would happen, I wanted him to know he could count on me. I spent hours talking to Chocolate. He got a new diet, more comfortable shoes, and I touched, massaged, and nuzzled him every day. He learned to bite an apple in half and relished munching carrots. Chocolate had the freedom to run, play, and roll in the dirt. At last he enjoyed being a horse.

Chocolate's coat grew shiny and his muscles became toned. He brought joy to my life and I brought a renewed spirit to his.

CARL HIBY

Lydia and Winter Chocolate

As we began to take short rides I realized I was educating a child who had never seen the world. Chocolate stopped at every landmark and awaited a detailed explanation. "That's a mailbox, Chocolate. We walk across the street because it is safe to cross in this manner," I prattled aloud as we walked along. Over time, Chocolate began to hold his head up. He became curious and more adventuresome. The more comfortable and trusting he became, the more willing he was to share his personality. The wonderful sense of humor that Chocolate had kept hidden, emerged. Chocolate taught me, once again, how important it is to remember that every animal is an individual, and how I must always honor and respect the spirit that resides within each one.

For years I had heard of Equitana, the most noted European horse event. Equitana USA fulfilled the dreams of horse lovers in the States by bringing to North America a showcase that the horse world had never experienced. At the core of this event is the belief that the future of the horse depends on an exchange of information and ideas from those within the industry. In 1997, Equitana USA planted its roots in the heart of horse country, Louisville, Kentucky.

The range of Equitana's offerings are vast, providing information on foreign breeds, herbal equine remedies, horse equipment, trail techniques, dressage, breed presentations, and jumping. The lectures are diverse as well, including my lecture aptly titled, "How Horses Communicate."

Truth be told, I get nervous before a lecture, but once those first few minutes pass it becomes a memorable experience. The audience makeup combines skeptics along with believers and those in between. They come from all walks of life, but it is their love of horses that binds them together. The biggest compliment I received was from a gentleman who approached me at the end of my lecture. Admitting that his wife literally dragged him in to hear me, he said my comments touched him and that it changed forever his perception of horses. He no longer doubted his strong feelings for horses. Another man, tears in his eyes, caught up with me as I left and whispered that he always knew the promises he had made to his dog immediately before the dog died, were understood.

In addition to giving lectures at Equitana. I also gave hours of consultations with horses and their owners. Janet Paxton, owner of Paxton Farms, asked me to speak to her horse, Picaro. She was curious to know if he was content with his life and work. At that time I had no idea that Picaro was honored by being chosen to represent the Hanoverian breed at Equitana. Janet accompanied me to Picaro's stall, and I was introduced to Picaro's trainer, Tim, who smiled, as he courteously but bluntly declared he was a skeptic. Assuring Tim that I understood and fully respected his position, I proceeded to meet Picaro, who greeted me warmly as I asked permission to enter his stall.

When I began to talk to Picaro, the first information he shared was that his *mom* (referring to Janet) *bought the farm for me!* Janet nodded explaining that she had met Picaro some time ago and wanted so much to own him, but didn't have the space or facility at the time. However, she promised Picaro they would one day be together. Janet purchased a farm and the following spring, purchased Picaro. The conversation continued with Picaro jumping from one topic to another, telling me details of his life. *Not long ago I enjoyed grapes. I really like my trainer and I was second best at my last barn. I like being top horse and at this farm I am number one!* Picaro showed me mental images of a blond female rider at the last place and stated, *I was not emotionally attached to her.* Picaro explained further, *Only Tim and a fair-complexioned child ride me now.* Janet confirmed that the child was her daughter and corroborated all the other information as well.

Picaro continued, *Sometimes I want mom to ride me—she won't ride me—that upsets me.* Janet admitted she hadn't ridden Picaro because she feared doing something incorrectly while riding him, and potentially causing a problem in Picaro's training. This was Janet's dream horse and she wanted everything just right for him. Janet promised that Picaro could take her for a ride, as long as Tim was there to supervise.

Picaro also told me of a breeding he had with a light-colored mare. He referred to her as an old mare and showed me a somewhat common-looking female horse, her muzzle slightly gray. Being quite elegant himself, Picaro was not thrilled with her but she was so smitten with him that he mellowed and was flattered. By the time I relayed this detail, Janet was wide eyed and Tim, the trainer, was hiding a grin, shaking his head. Janet validated this information explaining that Picaro had been bred with an unregistered mare as a test breeding.

My conversation with Picaro ended by my doing a body scan to search for any physical ailments. His overall health felt good. However, I cautioned that he had sinus problems and allergies (Janet nodded) and that he was extremely sensitive to chemicals. I also felt that the last upper tooth on each side of Picaro's mouth needed to be checked by a dentist. To this comment Tim responded immediately, saying that he had just called the dentist because he knew there was a problem. Picaro had been playing with his bit while he was being ridden. Then the trainer gave me a funny look, as if wondering, *How did she know that?*

On the third day of Equitana Janet voiced concern that Picaro appeared exhausted. Apparently, his night stall was on an end where he saw no one yet he heard loud noises from the nearby airport. The sounds of the planes frightened Picaro since he was used to country quiet and the music of crickets. Janet knew Picaro had not laid down to rest because he had no shavings on his body in the morning. I suggested that Janet sit down on the clean shavings in Picaro's stall, tell him it was safe, and that someone would check on him during the night. I also encouraged Janet to give Picaro permission to lie down and rest. The next morning Janet greeted me saying, "He was covered with shavings!" Picaro looked well rested and much happier. Janet repeated this reassuring communication for the next two nights with the same results. She was surprised and relieved that her message got across to Picaro. It validated her concern to care for him completely and that she could do this herself.

As Equitana ended, one more question about Picaro surfaced. This time the question came from the skeptic, Tim. He wanted to know how Picaro felt about going to the next Olympics to compete in the dressage division. Picaro's response was, *I would do it for you but planes make me nervous. I didn't like the long plane ride I took to get here.* Resolving Picaro's insecurities about such a plane trip was accomplished by simply explaining what was involved and reassuring him that Tim would be in charge. Picaro was certainly capable of understanding. If he does compete in the next Olympics those watching will have a treat as they observe a horse float gracefully through dressage.

In return I asked Tim, still a skeptic, how he felt about Picaro's comments. Tim answered that he would always be dubious but that the information about Picaro's teeth and the breeding mare were extremely accurate. Surprisingly, Tim ended up recommending my skills as an animal communicator to others. I considered this a huge compliment from a disbeliever. His parting words to me were, "I gave Picaro the grapes!"

At my horse lectures, I share what I call "inherited background and common breed characteristics." There are hundreds of breeds of horses, but for the lecture I highlight the most common. This seems to create a greater understanding of what motivates a particular horse. My assessments of horses based on breed characteristics and my experiences in communicating with them are along the following:

Arabians can be very snooty when I first talk to them. Being extremely self-sufficient, they may respond, *Oh, I don't know if I want to talk to you. I only talk to my owner. I picked her out. She understands me and that's all that I care about.*

Morgans, bred in colonial America, are family horses. A Morgan may say, *I am very versatile. Dad takes me to horse shows and the kids ride me and I can pull a cart.* They enjoy talking, are easy going, and love being around people.

Quarter Horses are fun because they are mellow, succinct and hard working. Known as another American breed and as a true cowboy horse, I have been told by Quarter Horses, *Yeah lady, I chased some cows. It's okay. It gave me something to do.* They are sweet and wonderful.

Thoroughbreds are known for being sensitive as if they wear their heart on their sleeve. A typical remark from a Thoroughbred might be, *Oh my God, the world is coming to an end. My owner's taking me to a jumping clinic and I don't know what to do!*

Although racehorses are not a breed (most of the racehorses I communicate with are Thoroughbreds) I include them within the lecture because I am continually asked about them. A lot of people want to take me to a race track because they think I can pick who's going to win. However, most horses think they are supposed to win the race. Yet, it is interesting from the horses' perspectives because when the gates open a variety of their individual experiences become apparent. With a novice racehorse, it is often a case of, *Why are we all running? Okay, I'll follow you.* The older, more experienced horses know what is going on and say, *I'm a pro.* Some horses say, *I have to go on the outside—so here we go again!* Other horses question, *Why do I have to do this?* And there are horses who are thrilled with racing, and say, *Wow this is fun! Look at all the people!* Still others are fearful, *I'd better be first to get to the finish line or I'm going to be in big trouble.*

One racehorse owner asked me to talk to her horse at River Down in Ohio. That afternoon he was racing in the prestigious Breeders Cup. Before the race I spoke to her about the horse's career and she explained he had never won a race until recently. All of a sudden he started to win and she wanted an explanation of what was responsible. I asked the horse and he visualized for me an event that took place after a race in which he finished last. The horse's groom was cooling him out by walking him around the back of the stable area. As the horse walked he became aware that another racehorse had died (of a heart attack) and he saw the horse's body being pulled out from the stall. The groom whispered, teasing, "If you don't run, this is what's going to happen to you!" After the owner relayed this story to the groom, he gasped, "Oh my goodness, I didn't know the horse understood any of that, but you're correct, because right after that the horse started winning!"

In addition to particular breed characteristics, it is also important to understand three basic categories for all horses: Cold Blooded, Warm Blooded, or Hot Blooded. These terms are associated with the geographical area, and more so the climate, from which the particular horse descended. There is a commonality of traits within each classification, sometimes physical and oftentimes personality and disposition.

Cold Bloods, as their name depicts, hail from cold climates found in Northern Europe and Canada. Many of the breeds originated in the Scandinavian countries of Norway, Denmark, Sweden, and Finland. These horses are known for being heavy boned with lots of feathering on the leg. Cold Bloods are large and strong, and were primarily work horses who labored in severe weather conditions. Personality traits for Cold Bloods include mellow and easy going. Some of the better known Cold Bloods include the Draft horse and the Thoroughbred.

Hot Bloods originated in Africa and Egypt where the mercury soars and the sun blazes. In order to endure the extreme heat, the horses in this group have a bone structure that is much lighter and more refined than that of the Cold Bloods. The personality trait most commonly associated with Hot Bloods is one of incredible stamina and high energy. The Arabian is an example of a Hot Blood.

The Warm Bloods evolved by breeding a Cold Blood with a Hot Blood. Some horse owners refer to the Warm Bloods as the best of both worlds. Many horse owners believe the personality of a Warm Blood is unbeatable. They are usually easy going, a temperament passed on from the Cold Blood. The Warm Blood likely will remain mellow and can be pushed further for endurance in competition. The Warm Bloods include many popular breeds, among them the Hanoverian, Trakehner, Holsteiner, Oldenburg, Danish and Swedish Warm Bloods. Many of these breeds, featured in major competitions like the Olympics, are recognized for their sturdiness under pressure.

Horses share similarities besides the obvious physical characteristics. Sadly, they share problems. The original horses were actually three-toed animals, the size of a large dog. Over time, with the help of evolution and breeding, their appearance has been altered to the horse we recognize today—a large animal supported by long legs and small hooves.

One serious downside of evolution and breeding is the horse's inability to regurgitate. The intestine measures thirty-three feet long, and because horses have been bred to be larger, their necks have grown longer proportionately. These characteristics can create a life-threatening situation because a horse cannot vomit. If a horse could vomit, the way a cat or a dog does, the colic problems horses suffer would be lessened to a large degree. However, colic problems have worsened with evolution and breeding, as well as the simple ability to burp. Only once in my life did I hear a horse burp and it was such a surprise. A horse owner's dreaded nightmare is a diagnosis of colic. Often surgery is necessary and a total recovery is questionable. Unfortunately, some horses are plagued by bouts of colic all of their lives, while others never experience its wrath.

Although it is generally accepted that emotional, physical, and environmental conditions factor into this illness, it is not known why some horses suffer from colic and others do not.

Horses are acutely perceptive. To protect them from predators, they have an early-warning system. With eyes positioned on the side of the head, horses have a panoramic field of vision. They can scan the horizon 340 of the 360 degrees around them. The disadvantage of this visual ability is that there are two narrow blind spots with which horses must contend: one directly in front of them and the other directly behind. Since horses cannot see what is directly in front of them at extremely close range, they are startled by someone who approaches head on. Horses can focus ahead in the distance and therefore, they must remember or memorize what they see in order to recall the image when they approach the obstacle— whether it is a jump, a stream, or a person.

Horses have frontal vision, as well as peripheral vision. This is called binocular vision. (When I communicate with horses I will often ask them to first tell me what they see in front of them, and then I ask what they see to the sides in their peripheral vision. It is astounding that an animal can keep this information straight!) In addition, horses' acute hearing helps protect them by virtually following what the eyes see. Each ear works inde- pendently and while the right ear might be standing straight, pinpointing data that the horse sees in the distance, the left ear may seemingly look as though it swiveled to the side while it attempts to locate information relevant to what the left eye is observing. All the senses work together to alert and protect the horse from the threat of danger.

⟶

By nature, horses are social and communicate with each other by scent, touch, and calling verbally. They greet one another by breathing into each other's nostrils. Humans have been successful in training these magnificent animals, not because we overpower them, but because they consider humans honorary members of the herd.

Horse lovers are well aware that each horse has individual needs. My work with animals over the years has illuminated this understanding time and again. Buster the Jumper was one horse who had some very specific needs. The first meeting I had with Buster and his owner, Marlene, was ten years ago at Oregon State University. Buster was a black-and-white Paint horse, impressive in stature. Marlene brought both of her horses, Secret and Buster, for the consultation. Secret, a dark-bay Thoroughbred, was Marlene's focus for the consultation, and Buster basically came along for the ride. Admitting that she initially bought Buster with the intent of selling him, Marlene elaborated that once she sold Buster she could not stop thinking about him. Six months later Buster's new owner, still unable to deal with such an unruly animal, offered him for sale and Marlene seized the opportunity to purchase Buster a second time. Buster remained obnoxious, tense, and reared constantly, all of his old habits still intact. Marlene tried a variety of training methods but to no avail.

Ironically, Buster's registered name was "Second In Command," since he was second to Secret. Marlene expected to succeed to the top of amateur owner jumpers with Secret and perhaps, beyond. She did not have similar expectations for Buster, and thus, he received less attention from Marlene.

When Buster was brought out to meet me for the consultation, his first comment was, *I've been watching you from my stall all day!* With that said, he slammed his hoof on my foot, asking, *Are you going to make me get off?* I waited a moment and with my hand gently pushed him off. Buster was completely confused by my calm but firm response. Easily I read his thoughts, *That's different–she didn't go wild and get angry—what happened?* I began talking to Buster and discovered that the only time Buster got attention was when he did something wrong. Years of negative behavior brought attention and excitement, much of which was amusing to Buster.

Marlene, having witnessed Buster step on my foot, waited for my reaction and my solution. Putting myself in Buster's situation enabled me to devise a plan and ultimately solve this problem. I explained that if he were mine, I would buy a fifty-pound bag of carrots and every time the "stinker" stood still I would give him one carrot and praise his good behavior. Simply standing still was good behavior and worthy of a carrot. So a carrot and praise became the rewards. Marlene's follow-up report after the consultation was that two days later half of Buster's negative behavior had ceased and by the end of the week all of his obnoxious antics had stopped. Buster was so busy chewing carrots he hardly had time to consider obnoxious behavior. This once rowdy animal, now safe and worthy of keeping, became a pleasure to be around. Reinforcement for positive behavior was the solution.

If the story ended here, the outcome would be considered quite satisfactory. However, Buster had a surprise for Marlene, his own well-kept secret. Marlene admittedly does not remember exactly when she discovered Buster's jumping ability, but one day he just started jumping. They have been jumping together for the past ten years. A few years after that consultation, Secret was retired. Marlene has bought three prospective replacement horses for Buster, expecting him to burn out as he aged. However, all three have been sold as Buster continues to jump. Buster has carried Marlene over adult amateur courses, Mini Grand Prix courses, and hunter, equitation, and medal courses for the past seven years. Most of them, Marlene confesses, have been ridden with her eyes shut tight while she hangs onto his mane. She concedes that no matter how badly she might misguide Buster up in front of a jump, he still jumps confidently. If Buster believes the jump will be disastrous, he politely and gently stops with his head up so Marlene will not fall off.

Once in awhile an animal comes along and knocks my socks off. This was the case with Beerzy, who became a regular client about eleven years ago. It has been a highlight of my career as an animal communicator to get to know Beerzy so well, and all of his likes and dislikes. He is quite a character with a personality that defies any notion of him "just being a horse." His registered name is Hobobred, but he dislikes this formal name because he is no "hobo," thus the nickname. "The Beerz," as he prefers to think of himself, is a Quarter Horse. He regards himself as number one to everybody simply because he is!

Mary owned the horse's mother and bred her, selling her piano to pay the stallion owner for his breeding fee. Beerzy was the result. My first visit with Beerzy remains the most memorable. When Beerzy communicated what he wanted, I laughed as I relayed the message to Mary. The horse told me, *I want you to know that I really like birthday parties! I like wearing hats and I think it's funny to have confetti hanging all over my head.* Continuing, Beerzy recounted, *Not everyone who was supposed to be at my last birthday party was there on time.* It was true. Both of Beerzy's trainers promised to be there to share in the festivities, but showed up toward the party's end. In spite of the disappointment, there were wonderful moments.

The entire barn turned out for Beerzy's birthday party and all the horses were invited. One of the horses, tall and gray, appropriately named Platinum, was owned by a couple so strict and regimented that their horse had never tasted birthday cake. Beerzy said, *I am so happy that Platinum came to my party and got to know how horses should live instead of just being a vehicle for people!* Another time Mary combined a birthday party for Beerzy and King, another horse member of the family. King had great fun and was the life of the party. On the other hand, Beerzy's behavior was bizarre. Thinking he was sick, Mary called me for a consultation. "Beerzy is not sick, he's mad," I explained. "He had to share his birthday party with King."

Beerzy, at first steel dapple gray in color, has lightened with age. He is noticeably irritated and will snort with disgust when simply referred to as white. His hair coat, although previously considered unique for a Quarter Horse, is now desired and horses are specifically bred for this trait. At age twenty-two, Beerzy now prefers to hang out in the house rather than the barn. Since his stable is just behind the house he has quite matter of factly walked through the open back door of the house—appearing in the living room as though it were a natural occurrence. Beerzy likes to go everywhere and do everything. He is comfortable in a downtown parade, in a show ring, or in the mountains. It seems as though the world was made for him. Mary admits that throughout the county she is known simply as "Beerzy's mother."

When Beerzy was in training for jumping he was often stabled away from home. During one consultation, Mary asked what Beerzy wanted for Christmas. In no uncertain terms, Beerzy communicated that he wanted a purple blanket just like the one worn by the horse across from him. That was Watson, who indeed did have a purple blanket, long before purple was fashionable. Beerzy, having numerous blankets, did not need another, but after many phone calls and a lot of leg work, a purple blanket was found. Beerzy also acquired purple shipping boots and a purple halter. In time, Beerzy became saturated with purple. (See Questions and Answers in the back of the book for more information on animals seeing in color. I do believe that animals see all primary colors, although this is scientifically disputed.)

Although there have been a variety of entertaining and thoughtful conversations with horses over the years, the most important conversations relate to medical issues. At one point Beerzy was put on antibiotics for a runny nose and a slight cough. Thinking that his lungs might be affected, the veterinarian suggested that Beerzy be hand walked instead of ridden. After the third round of antibiotics, with no improvement, Mary called me. Communicating briefly with Beerzy, I asked Mary, "Have you refinished anything in the barn? Anything that smells like paint thinner or stain or something like that? Beerzy's allergic to that and he's having a very hard time breathing the fumes." As it turns out, a friend of Mary's was restoring a sailboat tiller, using a water protective varnish. The tiller was hung over the rafters in the barn for the final stages of the drying process. After removing it, Beerzy's illness cleared up immediately.

A good trainer is like a good teacher, two eyes in the front, two eyes in the back—and always aware. This was Kris, manager of a racehorse barn, who invited me to consult with ten racehorses. My primary purpose was to "discuss" racing issues with these horses, but Kris sensed uncharacteristic behavior with three of her horses, and had been unable to figure out the cause.

When I arrived at the barn, I was taken to meet the first of the three "problems." Roscoe, Kris's personal horse, was a dark chestnut Quarter Horse. He was a pony horse with a very specific job. It is the duty of the pony horse to lead the racehorse up to the starting gate, keeping the racehorse calm and quiet.

The second problem horse, Queenie, a racehorse, was a three-year old refined Thoroughbred mare. Considered the star of the barn, Queenie was reserved and aloof. Light chestnut with a thin white blaze, Queenie was a stakes horse and ran for big money. If Queenie were a star in a 1940s movie she would have been considered a "classy dame."

Third, was Oscar, a dark mahogany bay, who had been imported from Europe. Oscar reminded me of a retired prize fighter with healed-over gashes, dents, and lumps. He had been abused. When Kris bought Oscar, his health was poor and his confidence nonexistent. Kris nurtured Oscar body and soul, and was responsible for his return to racing—a comeback of sorts.

Once I met all three horses, I needed to get specifics from the horses themselves. I began with the star, Queenie. This horse was smart. Easily picking up her feelings of stardom, I mentally asked her what her life was like. She showed me a jockey riding her to the finish line—applause—screaming—winning. She further explained, *It doesn't matter who rides me. I do it the same way all the time—like a lady—clean and spiffy.* She ended with, *I am the star of the barn!* I asked Queenie to show me how she wins each race "the same way" and she visualized breaking from the gate in the back of the pack. Waiting for the rest of the horses to wear themselves out a little bit. Then going around the outside and galloping at top speed and winning! I verbally dialogued this visualization for Kris. She drew in her breath and uttered, "That's exactly how Queenie wins every race."

Before leaving Queenie, I asked her to tell me what her feelings were for Roscoe. Very demurely she conveyed to me an emotional sense that she felt in love with him. However, she told me she takes her job seriously, and it comes first. Indeed, she does—Queenie won the 1998 Breeders Cup!

When I met with Roscoe, he immediately told me that he thought it very humorous that any horse had to run for a living, (earn hay) while all he had to do was walk the fancy racehorse to the gate and then he'd be finished with work. He visualized the racehorses waking early, (their first workout was from 6 to 9:00 AM) but his workday began much later at 3:00 PM. Quite proud of himself, Roscoe summed up the consultation by telling me, *Look at those stupid racehorses—they have to run all the way around—and I'm done.* Queenie was just another racehorse to him, nothing more.

Oscar, poor Oscar, was very possessive of Queenie. Everything seemed difficult for him. If I could sense that a horse was dyslexic, having to learn everything backwards, this was the horse. This was not a bad attitude that I picked up, but rather a feeling that I can describe only as a learning disability. Kris validated that this was true. Oscar showed me pictures of his life in Europe—sad pictures. He did not want to dwell on it. He had started to win and do well and then his images changed and I saw him frightened and scared. Again I noticed his badly marked body and felt how he had been abused. Oscar just loved Queenie and he visualized himself following her, walking beside her, patiently waiting, and believing they would be together. After the consultation, it became clear that the three problem horses were the result of a love triangle!

Sadly, many animals are forced to do things they do not want to do. They have no choice. There are mares who are destined to be bred over and over again with care given only to their physical well-being while their emotional needs are never considered. Unfortunately, this is the situation when an animal is solely viewed as a financial investment.

Katie is someone who tunes into her horse's emotional state, and she had a gut feeling that something was wrong with her mare, Memory. There were no physical problems, yet Katie felt that something was wrong. Katie always planned to breed Memory, a stunning horse, and keep her baby. This way she would have the second horse she dreamed of owning. As this strategy was about to come to fruition, Katie continued to feel that something wasn't right. She was skeptical of animal communicators but decided to call me because she wanted to understand what was wrong.

When I met with Katie and Memory, the horse communicated immediately and directly. Memory told me that she did not want to have a baby and that was that! She had no interest in raising a foal and no motivation to lose her magnificent figure. (Memory was keenly aware of her physical beauty because she picked up these feelings from her owner.) For Memory, losing her figure was a negative, since she had a fit and toned body much like a human athlete. Animals accept each other for who they are and see beyond the physical—but that does not prevent an animal from being vain.

Memory saw no reason to go through this ordeal only to please her owner. She also broadcast her feelings to other horses in the stable and when I communicated with them, they disclosed the same information. I told Katie that if she really wanted Memory to have a baby for her, basically she had to bargain with the horse, making many promises before attempting to breed her. Katie ended up with a beautiful filly, but not before promising Memory vast amounts of time together trail riding. Memory was a good mother for as short a time as nature deemed necessary, until the filly could be on her own. This is the one horse that I believe would have hired a "nanny" if she could have!

In 1992, I was contacted by Beverly whose horse, Omner, a seventeen-year old Arabian had been diagnosed with a fast-spreading cancer, and later had a miraculous recovery. The year before an ultrasound showed a football-size mass above Omner's left kidney. Two biopsies confirmed sarcoma. His enzyme values were extremely poor, and the prognosis was depressing because surgery would not be effective. Expecting him to go down hill quickly, Beverly was determined to keep Omner comfortable and euthanize him when the time came. Another horse owner suggested that Beverly give Omner some supplements, a combination of herbs, vitamins, minerals, and enzymes. Beverly faithfully

BEVERLY GRAY

Bravo feeding Omner his grain when Omner was sick.

administered the supplements, and in addition adjusted the type of hay and grain he ate. At times Beverly felt helpless to change the situation. Omner had lost a dramatic amount of weight and it was heartbreaking to watch her horse waste away.

A friend offered a grave site on her farm, and Beverly even decided which halter Omner would be buried in. However, after several weeks on the supplements Omner began to gain weight. Two months later Omner was chasing his horse companion around the pasture. Another ultrasound showed that the tumor had regressed to the size of an orange. Several months later, there was no trace of the tumor.

Beverly contacted me, even though she was skeptical, because she wanted another confirmation of Omner's well-being. Although Beverly felt secure about the results of the negative ultrasound, she needed validation that Omner felt as good as she believed he did. When I began the consultation over the phone I knew nothing of the situation, so I began as always, asking the animal's name, breed, and location. The first information I picked up was that Omner had been severely ill, and I felt the pain he had once felt on his left side. Assuring Beverly that Omner felt fine now, I returned to the time

Beverly selected him as a yearling, and his lack of confidence as a youngster. Omner sent a feeling of being jealous of any other horse Beverly spent time with. Then, Omner changed the subject by showing me that his favorite color was purple. Interestingly, Beverly had just outfitted him in purple because she liked the color. He showed me images of running up and down hills, through water, and loving the trail rides. I felt endurance riding was still very much a part of Omner's life and a genuine possibility.

Beverly later consulted with the veterinarian who agreed that Omner was physically fit to resume endurance riding. Starting slowly in order to build up his stamina over a six-month period, Beverly and Omner worked together. Success has become reality. In 1997, "AA Omner" was awarded The Hall of Fame Trophy at the annual American Endurance Convention in Reno. With ten years of trail riding over eight thousand miles, one hundred and twenty-five competitions, forty-two wins, and eighteen best condition awards, Omner has set a record that few horses have matched.

Today, Omner's health regime consists of acupuncture, chiropractic adjustments, massage (T-Touch), and consultations to let me know how he's feeling. He complains every once in awhile, in particular about Bravo, the eight-year old Arabian who will follow in his footsteps. *Bravo needs to be motivated*, Omner told me. Beverly agrees. Omner has become verbal and nickers and whinnies as he communicates with his owner. His pasture is adjacent to the house and interaction with Beverly is constant from dawn to dusk. His world is a beautiful meadow with a log-rail fence and a view of snow-capped mountains in the distance. Today, Omner and Beverly are bonded by a deep-rooted and powerful spirit stemming from a life-threatening experience.

Another horse I worked with took a very different turn in his work after an accident that severely affected the owner. Stephanie teaches dressage and her husband, Dave, is a farrier. They needed help concerning their Arabian stallion, who was their first stallion and their first show horse. Millennium's name was shortened to "Mill," and then somehow it changed to "Mel." He wound up being called Mel Gibson because he is a very handsome horse, somewhat cocky, and extremely sure of himself.

The owners called me because of a serious accident. Three months earlier Mel threw Stephanie, sending her to the hospital with a concussion and a broken collar bone. Stephanie provided the only details she remembered—Mel threw his head up, he then lunged forward, and fell on his right shoulder with Stephanie still in the saddle. My job was to find out why this happened.

When I met with Mel he pictured Stephanie riding him. He communicated to me, *She is asking me to do dressage that I haven't learned.* After Mel told me this, I felt pain in my neck as if something had been pulled. Then I visualized a vertebrae out in Mel's neck. Apparently, the vertebrae put pressure on a nerve, which must have caused the horse to black out and fall. I felt this animal's confusion and his upset. Mel knew he had done something to his "mom" but was unsure of what happened. Stephanie was devastated because she felt that this horse, the love of her life, had hurt her.

Stephanie's healing was slow, so in the interim Mel was sent to another trainer with the intention of teaching him Western Pleasure to compete in the show ring. Stephanie decided to sell the horse, thinking she could never be close to Mel again. She hurt both physically and emotionally. After three weeks with the other trainer, Mel got extremely depressed and Stephanie was contacted. Again, Stephanie called me asking what Mel was thinking.

Mel communicated to me that he knew he was being punished and accepted it, but he was terrified of being sold. *Please give me another chance—a second chance*, he told me. At her husband's urging, Mel was brought home. Dave went trail riding with Mel while Stephanie recovered. And as she healed, her compassion emerged. Although Stephanie gave up dressage because of her injury, she kept Mel. "I ride with a wonderful trainer and of all things, Western Pleasure in reining," wrote Stephanie in a recent note. "The loose rein and relaxed attitude is what Mel wanted. My friend is much happier, and I love this boy. Thank you for your help a year ago."

Over the years I have continued to be humbled by the depth of emotion and the variety of personality characteristics all animals are capable of. This final horse story is amazing to me, not so much because of what the horse, Elvira, communicated to me, but because of the strength of her character. Elvira was a survivor and she knew it and lived it.

I was invited for two days of consultations at a training facility in Southern California. The barn was home to one hundred pleasure and show horses. The owners, John and Katie, made their horses the focus of their life work. Part of their job was to find and assess new horses for clients. Elvira was a black Thoroughbred who had been transported on a truck from Texas on consignment. The arrangement was for a two-week trial, at the end of which any or all horses not being bought would return by truck to Texas.

Katie wanted to buy Elvira for her husband, John, but hesitated because the horse "looked like a bag of bones, and had a wild look in her eye." Katie also sensed that the horse had lived through a trauma. Timing was not on Katie's side. She was not at the barn when the truck arrived a half day early, and loaded Elvira for the return to Texas. As soon as she realized Elvira was gone, Katie contacted the dispatcher and learned the truck's route. In haste she headed out in her pickup truck with no thought about what she would do when she caught up with them. Although Katie caught up with the truck in Utah, the driver did not have permission to release Elvira, and Katie was forced to follow them all the way back to Texas.

Once in Texas, Katie purchased the horse, borrowed a horse trailer and drove the long road back home. When Katie presented her husband with what she hoped to be the gift of a lifetime, his initial assessment of Elvira was anything but positive. The horse looked out of condition and John wondered if Elvira was capable of jumping at all. However, on their first ride together, Elvira cleared four-foot and then five-foot jumps with ease. John was shocked that he misjudged Elvira's ability, so he listened with an open mind as Katie pleaded to look beyond the "ugly" horse he saw.

Katie felt that beyond the unkempt coat, and the out-of-condition body was a huge loving heart. Katie continued to believe in Elvira's goodness even when the horse's bad behavior became the talk of the stable. Elvira lunged at people walking past, trying to bite them, and she was difficult with the grooms when they came to clean her stall.

By the time I met Elvira her coat was glossy, she looked fit, self-assured, and clearly in love with her "dad," Dave. Elvira's stall was first on the aisle, a special location, and she saw herself as "barn manager." She got to watch all the activity or what I call "horse TV." When we began communicating, Elvira willingly shared her past, showing me pictures of Katie following the truck to Texas. I felt Elvira was touched by Katie's kindness.

However, I had also sensed her dark side when we first met, so I asked Elvira to show me what her life was like before the ride from Texas. She visually showed me that she had once raced. Then I saw her limping, and I felt her pain and learned that she had sustained an injury to her rear-fetlock joint. This type of injury, which is caused by constant pounding, is considered to be a serious sports injury, and often summons the end of a career.

Elvira also communicated that she was uncooperative during three breeding attempts in the past. She was hobbled (her rear legs tied) and drugged. None of the breedings were successful. The message Elvira repeated over and over was, *I'm a survivor. Don't cry for me.* Katie later validated the breeding information from someone who knew Elvira in Texas.

When I left the consultation with Elvira, I was moved, and inspired, by the realization that animals, like people, can rise above extreme adverse conditions. Katie and John continue to care for Elvira and everyone at the barn has come to revere her. Canyon, the horse across the aisle, has become Elvira's friend. Elvira sees Canyon as the "king," while Canyon sees Elvira as the "queen." Now, Elvira greets every new horse arrival reassuring them, *This barn is a good place and a safe place.*

Cire the Iguana

Chapter Six

FOREIGN WORLDS

In whose hand is the soul of every living thing,
and the breath of all mankind.

– JOB 12:10

When I think of exotic animals, I consider that to mean creatures who would not usually be found in domestic settings. I find them intriguingly unusual. Exotic animals who are kept as animal companions are so rare that most individuals have little or no contact with them. For this reason, people may be timid and uncomfortable in their presence. As an animal communicator, I have felt both unprepared and uncomfortable upon an initial meeting with an exotic animal. Nevertheless, as familiarity and friendships have evolved, some of these animals have invited me into their world, and it has been challenging and fulfilling.

When I met Pearl, the owner of exotic cats, my life was enriched beyond comprehension. We connected immediately and over the years I have become acquainted with several exotic cats Pearl has taken home. She acquired her first cats before protective regulations were in place. In 1968, it was legal to purchase Ocelots and Bobcats from pet stores. Pearl acquired a Northern Bobcat, Sheba, and an Ocelot, Samelita, in this manner. The two cats were spayed and since then have lived harmoniously with one another, and are wonderful animal companions.

Around this time several key events affected Pearl's life even further. The late Bill Hodge, a Disney animal trainer, taught Pearl about the bond between an owner and Ocelot; a bond so exceptionally strong that if the animal's owner dies, the Ocelot would more than likely die shortly thereafter. It was also through Hodge that Pearl became aware of the need to provide rescue homes for these cats. There were young cats whose mothers had been killed by hunters. Exotic cats bought in pet stores were often declawed and defanged before their owners decided to dispose of them, making their return to the wild an impossibility. Pearl's home became a sanctuary and her name was added to the list of willing rescuers.

Pearl joined The Long Island Ocelot Club, an organization that has since changed its name to The Long Island Ocelot Club Endangered Species Conservation Federation Inc. The objectives of the group are to educate and assist private exotic cat owners in raising their animals to be healthy and sound. The name change reflects the effort made to recognize the severe situation faced by animals on the endangered list and the need to eradicate the crisis. Pearl holds permits from The Department of Agriculture and The Department of Fish and Wildlife. While laws vary from state to state, the cats who reside with Pearl do so legally, but she is aware that this is a sensitive subject wrought with extreme emotion.

At present, five exotic cats live under Pearl's roof. Tisha and Brandy are Bobcats, a female and male respectively. The Ocelots, all females, are Carmelita, Scarlet, and Baby. The two species of cats differ greatly in appearance. The Ocelots are quite small, under thirty pounds, and have an average length tail and resemble a miniature Jaguar. Most wild Ocelots are from South America, but a few still roam wild as far north as Mexico and Texas. The facial stripes, called rosettes, are the same as those found on their larger relatives. Body fur remains the same length throughout the year and is marked exquisitely. The Ocelot's skin directly under each marking mimics the pattern exactly. Ears are furry and are softly rounded on top.

BONNIE S. WEINTRAUB

Baby, the Ocelot   *Brandy, the Bobcat*

In contrast, the Bobcat weighs about thirty-five pounds and the fur adjusts with the seasons, short during the summer, and longer and fuller in winter. A Bobcat's tail is short, only between four and seven inches long. Bobcat ears have furry little tufts that stick straight up into the air and resemble antennae. Each cat has a distinctive personality and yet these wild animals are able to live together in harmony, respecting each other—a lesson humans are still attempting to master.

In addition to being breathtakingly beautiful, these exotic cats have emotions that are more visible and seem to go deeper than those of a domestic cat. Their wildness is more apparent when they express emotion and instinctively react. They will treat humans just like any other animal, and will not monitor themselves, including quick swats with their sizable paws. I quickly learned to always pay attention when in the company of these exotic cats.

The bond between Pearl and her cats is intense—mentally, spiritually—and nurturing. Pearl believes that her life's purpose is to care for the cats. Undoubtedly, the events that have taken place to make this possible have been no accident at all. When asked what the cats have taught her, she responds softly, "What a wonderful world this is. We people are too busy to see it, but the animal kingdom is a wonderful world."

Pearl lives with her cats—they don't live with her. There is a very big difference. From this belief and lifestyle comes her philosophy that the language of exotics cannot be understood until one has lived among them. Trust overrides instinct and these cats are totally dependent on Pearl for all of their needs. The biggest problem that wild animals face once they trust a human hand is that they become dependent. However, if it were not for human intervention, the animals placed in this woman's care would not have survived. Survival behaviors are taught by the mother cat from the moment of birth. A human's lessons cannot substitute for the training a mother cat provides. And no cat can survive in the wild without claws and fangs. Without this natural defense, the cat would be easy prey. The reality is life in a sanctuary, and Pearl's cats continue to thrive. They are free to move throughout the house and have total access to the outdoors—the lush natural grounds of her secured property.

Most often Pearl calls on my communication skills to determine the problem before the vet attempts to treat the animal. For years we have worked hand in hand. Not everything is serious, and as imagined, there are hilarious stories.

The exotic cat I have known the longest is Branford Muffin, called Brandy for short. This Bobcat turned eighteen in 1998. When we first met, admittedly, I was very uncomfortable not knowing what to expect. Brandy would either walk behind the sofa following me with his eyes or walk directly behind me, shadowing my movements. When I met him, he smoothly walked past me, turned around, and popped me with his paw. As I recovered from this unexpected cuff, Pearl's husband assured me that Brandy did indeed like me a lot, and that this tap was merely a show of affection! Often I reflect on this incident when Pearl reminds me that although her cats are domesticated, they still maintain their wild instincts. In turn, I respect each cat and now feel honored whenever Brandy demonstrates his affection for me with a little swat of his paw!

Whenever my schedule permits I visit Pearl's home. On one such visit, Brandy was in the guest room while I showered. When

I got out of the shower, Pearl was amused to see me running down the hall screaming, "He ate my bra!" Indeed Brandy had and I held up a garment filled with holes for her to see. Pearl admitted that he had a "thing about eating bras" and he had eaten holes in several of hers as well. Pearl explained that this was the ultimate compliment—this meant Brandy accepted and loved me. Exotic cats are very particular about people and if the person is not with them on a day-to-day basis, they normally do not accept you easily. Honored that I was part of Brandy's club, I could enjoy the surprises that came forth from his bag of tricks.

One of the first medical situations that I encountered with Brandy was Pearl's call for help because Brandy kept opening and closing his mouth. He had been home alone and nothing seemed amiss, but something was definitely wrong with his mouth. Over the phone I connected with Brandy and felt something sharp caught in his mouth. As I worked with him, and "stepped into his body," I saw him swallow a red plastic tack, the kind used on a cork board. It was lodged behind his last back tooth, deep in the gum. Carefully, Pearl looked into his mouth and found the red plastic disc I described and contacted the vet. Considering this an emergency, since Brandy could have choked had it become dislodged, the vet came to the house with forceps and antibiotics, and removed the tack that night.

The smallest of the Ocelots is "Scarlet Miss Ferocia," Scarlet for short. She is the most demanding of all the exotic cats in the household, and is the only cat who has ever displayed what Pearl calls a hot temper. Extremely impatient, Scarlet knows the meaning of "now!" If Pearl hears Scarlet's dish move across the counter and does not respond, Scarlet will nudge it along a bit farther. This is Scarlet's way of communicating, *Food—now!* If Pearl does not respond quickly the dish ends up on the floor. Scarlet thrives on teasing the other cats and instigates play and tiffs. When Scarlet sits idly twitching her tail, she looks as if she is plotting what she'll do next.

On one occasion, typically healthy Scarlet appeared to be very uncomfortable. Pearl had no idea what was causing Scarlet to feel ill. The only indication that a problem existed was her odd chewing pattern. Normally a robust eater, Scarlet was exceedingly careful when chewing and Pearl noticed food shift to the left side of her mouth. Working again by phone, I felt a painful sore spot on the very top of Scarlet's upper-right gum. Pearl was then able to put Scarlet on her lap and check the Ocelot's gum, gently applying pressure to the upper right. Pearl found the sore spot and the vet was able to medicate the gum and clean her teeth. Once healed, Scarlet's personality returned intact.

⌒

The transition of communicating with a warm-blooded furry cat to communicating with a cold-blooded reptile is quite challenging. In the early years of my work as an animal communicator, I was insecure about the accuracy of my readings. Actually, even now, I wake up each morning wondering, *Can I nail it today?* I take nothing for granted. And I am grateful for every day that I can use my skills.

One day after completing a barn call, where I successfully talked to several horses, I breathed a huge sigh of relief. Only one year into my independent work as an animal communicator, I was still rather shaky, and glad the demanding day was over. I was proud that I had survived both the experience and my nerves. *Finally*, I thought, *I can relax.* However, the calm was short lived as Melissa, the owner's daughter, approached me holding a rather large, and antiquated type of cat carrier. Unable to see inside since the carrier was solid fiberboard dotted with air holes, I was totally unprepared to make David's acquaintance. David was Melissa's eight-foot long Boa Constrictor.

As the story unfolded, I learned that Melissa had taken care of her Boa Constrictor since he was a baby, and the snake had been quite ill for the past month and a half. David lived at college with Melissa, where a local veterinarian examined the snake. Unfortunately, the vet was stymied, explaining that reptiles normally go through a shed and proceed into dormancy. Although they usually resume eating once the shed is complete, David did not. Melissa's dad was convinced that I could get to the bottom of this, while Melissa, who was certainly concerned, wanted to know if I had ever worked with a snake. I admitted that I had not, but there is a first time for everything.

Returning to the tack room with Melissa and the snake, the number of observers increased as Melissa's mom and sister joined us. David took it in stride as he slithered around the expanse. I got quiet, pictured a college room, and visualized David in his tank. The unmistakable smell of paint made me wince. I questioned whether Melissa had painted her dorm room. Immediately, she volunteered that she had painted David's "hot rock," an electrically heated rock on which cold-blooded reptiles enjoy resting. Melissa admitted that she could faintly smell paint fumes when the rock was plugged in, although she had done the painting two months previously. I was certain that this was what made the snake sick.

By this time I began feeling quite queasy and explained that David was so nauseous from the smell of the paint that he was unable to eat. Melissa agreed to discard the painted rock and replace it with one made of natural stone. Her dad, quite pleased with what he had witnessed, requested that I continue inquiring about the rest of David's life.

Agreeing to try, I mentally put David back in his tank to get an idea of his life and three times I saw and felt blue satin sheets. I thought to myself, *This is crazy. There is no reason for it.* Not understanding where it was coming from, I finally told Melissa, "I am still new at this. You are my first reptile client and I don't know what this means, but I see and feel blue satin sheets." With that, her dad jumped in excitedly, explaining he had been to her dorm room and indeed Melissa had blue satin sheets on her bed. He added that David often slept in bed with her.

Once I regrouped, I asked David to show me other experiences that he shared with his owner. David pictured Melissa smuggling him into a movie hidden inside her bomber jacket. Quite pleased with himself, David had managed to spook several people. Melissa validated this, adding that it was *Psssst*, a movie about a snake, shown at the college campus.

The family was intrigued with these findings. Melissa's dad impatiently asked me what happened the day David got loose in the dormitory hall. He explained that Melissa had called home to relay the funny story, which actually wasn't funny at first because Melissa thought David was dead. Once again, I became David and put myself back into his tank. He immediately placed me on the bed. Looking around the room, I saw Melissa studying, while a bored David slid off the bed and headed down the hall. Within moments I heard the girls scream for Melissa to come and get David. Certain that something was wrong, the girls continued to scream, pleading with Melissa to check him. Melissa tore into the hall to discover that David was stretched out straight. He was motionless, and Melissa immediately thought David was dead. Now that I had the entire picture, I once again became David, and could see a line up of fuzzy slippers and socked feet. I felt the girls' agitation and saw fingers pointing. Silently, I asked David to explain. He responded, *I didn't know where that snake was, but I stayed real still!* As far as David was concerned, he was just a really tall guy in a leather suit, and he wondered where "the snake" was that everyone was talking about!

My communication with David paved the way for educating me about reptiles and their distinct personalities. Ultimately, another "guy in a leather suit" entered my life. I had flown to the East Coast to care for my mother, who was quite ill, and the only animal-related phone calls that I accepted were those considered emergencies. One such call came from a woman, Peg, who expressed panic as she admitted to being skeptical and scared. Her pet, Cire, was near death and the vet had nothing left to try. Could I help him?

The first bit of information I picked up was that this animal liked sweet potatoes, and confused by the data, I innocently asked, "What kind of dog likes sweet potatoes?" Quickly correcting me I learned that Cire (Eric spelled backwards) absolutely loved sweet potatoes but was not a dog! I came to learn that he was a

Honduran Iguana, bought as a three-inch long baby from a wholesaler. Peg had seen Cire among some one hundred and fifty other little wiggly Iguanas as he sat inside the aquarium looking directly at her. Three times Peg got the unmistakable feeling he was asking to be taken home. She picked him. Cire was raised with one dog and several cats, whose newborn kittens would nurse on his spines. Cire learned to use the litter box by following the cats, so it's no great surprise that he assumed he was either a cat or a dog with a long tail.

When Peg called me for a consultation, Cire had not eaten in three days and his skin felt dehydrated. Peg walked me through the recent veterinary findings, which were rather detailed. The first vet thought Cire was jaundiced because of his orange color. As it turns out, Honduran Iguanas are this unique color. (The year after Cire's purchase, Honduras ceased exporting Iguanas, thus many vets had never seen this particular species.) A blood test registering a high level of bilirubin indicated liver trouble. The second vet ordered a liver biopsy, which required an incision from chest to belly button. Miraculously, Cire healed, and Peg learned later that rarely do reptiles survive this type of surgery. Ironically, Peg selected an Iguana expressly because of the Iguana's long life span. She had always been an animal lover and had lost several beloved dogs. She considered a dog's life span too short, and felt confident this Iguana would spend a lot of quality time with her.

The third and last vet was extremely interested in learning about reptiles. An ultrasound provided the necessary information to determine that Cire's liver was not enlarged, but rather ulcerated. Healing his liver while increasing his immunity was a priority. The vet suggested sweet potato and vitamin C to start. At that time, very little was known about a diet for the adult Iguana although it is now accepted that this reptile cannot eat protein for its entire life. At maturity, somewhere between age two and three years, Iguanas become strictly vegetarian for survival reasons. Cire began to recover, yet there seemed to be something we were all missing.

After that consultation, we still didn't have an answer, but I thought about the situation constantly. Feeling that something environmental was involved, I agreed to make an atypical house call. Having no expectations, I entered the apartment and was greeted warmly by the dog, as Cire cruised over to meet me. It was impossible to ignore his bony fingers and long nails. Literally, I stood frozen, until I was told that Cire only wanted to follow me around and perhaps sit on my lap to say "thank you." (He now felt better and he "knew" I was there to help him.) Neither thrilled nor flattered, I felt much safer once Peg produced Cire's perch, onto which he eagerly climbed. It was easy to recognize my discomfort and he looked genuinely upset that I seemed afraid. My reaction caused Cire additional disappointment, for I, like many others, did not immediately acknowledge how wonderful and handsome he was.

The visit proved worthwhile. Observing the Iguana in his own home, I was not only able to "see" Cire lick the floor, but "smell" and "taste" the cleaning product used as well. Peg regularly washed the floor with a common household disinfectant in order to maintain a germ-free environment. It was the residue remaining on the floor, after rinsing, that I tasted and smelled. This verified my belief that there was a missing piece to the puzzle. As soon as Peg stopped using this cleaning product, Cire recovered fully. Once again, that gut feeling or hunch, too powerful to ignore, bore out my suspicion.

When Cire sits on his tree stand at a pet fair, he sits there by choice. Cire can climb down from his tree at any time because he is never restrained. It is as though he knows his job is to greet and educate the many passersby, and he takes the job seriously. At a pet show, he loves to sit on his tree and people watch—while humans, in turn, Iguana watch! He adores kids and is tolerant of little fingers touching and stroking him. Cire doesn't have to purr or wag a tail to make his feelings known. If he likes a curious admirer, he cocks his head, poses for photographs, and follows with his eyes. His fan club is filled with onlookers who like to feel his energy and touch his beaded skin. If there is a person he doesn't like, his feelings are easy to read, as he flexes his muscles and stands tall while glaring at him or her. Tactfully, the person is warned to watch out for Cire's tail. Iguanas use their tail to knock their enemy to the ground. His tail is as solid as a cable and as fierce as a bull whip.

The thermostat in a reptile tells the animal to shut down when the tempera- ture drops. The heat of the day, or the desert climate, allows a reptile to move around in comfort. In addition, Iguanas have a solar cell on the top of their head.

Cire

This acts like a light switch, which allows them to determine day from night. Cire accompanied me to a pet show in New York and his carrier was placed in a cool area of the airplane. By the time we arrived and settled into the hotel room, Cire needed to thaw out. Plugging in the hot rock, I felt his impatience, and turning around I found him hugging the radiator! Cire has been smuggled into hotels in a gym bag, which at nearly six feet long is quite an acrobatic achievement. If it is a worrisome situation, he will attempt to co-operate by pulling his tail all the way into the bag and remain very still.

As Cire aged, his behavior changed and he became aggressive. He began to approach his owner in a hostile fashion—mouth open with a threatening posture. Documentation on an adult male Iguana living in a human family situation was nonexistent; thus, Peg did not understand the shift in his personality. Cire had entered the throngs of breeding maturity. When this pubescent behavior was demonstrated, he was disciplined with tank time, and allowed the run of the house only under strict supervision. Although his behavior was natural, and totally acceptable in the wild, he was required to alter his conduct and learn self-control since he lived among humans. The difficulty in handling an

Iguana during this twice-yearly breeding season is the reason that most mature Iguanas are turned over to zoos.

Five years have passed and I remain involved in Cire's life. I depend on Cire's precise communication. Unlike a dog, who wags its tail to validate, Cire's messages have to be crystal clear to be understood. He has taught me that Iguanas, like all animals, have a presence and a personality as well as a tremendous sense of humor. He maintains a grace and patience when meeting the public. At one point, I asked Cire what he believed to be the purpose of his life. He answered me by saying, *I am a citizen of the universe. I am to educate people and teach respect.* I consider Cire to be an animal spirit filled with wisdom far beyond his chronological years. He is a true animal shaman.

Birds are another species who demonstrate a wonderful intelligence and capability for understanding. Contrary to common belief, birds, especially exotic birds, are not easy pets to care for. Their owners devote tremendous time and effort to create a healthy and happy environment for them. Cheryl is one such bird owner who is committed to caring for Lemon Drop, her Umbrella Cockatoo. I was surprised to learn that although Cheryl brought her bird home at ten weeks of age, she actually purchased Lemon Drop from a breeder who allowed the prospective owner to buy an egg prior to hatching.

Lemon Drop is a magnificent white Cockatoo with bright lemon yellow under her crest, wings, and tail. She has blue rims around her eyes and jet black eyes, feet, and beak. Birth announcements broadcasted her arrival in 1988 and her egg shell sits in a glass jar on Cheryl's desk. An annual birthday party celebrates the date of "hatching." It was at one such birthday party that Cheryl received a gift certificate for a consultation with me. The consultation was given by a work friend who previously had me talk to two cats. The friend was aware that Lemon Drop was having some problems.

"Lemon," as she prefers to be known, was experiencing an over-preening problem, commonly known as feather plucking. Causes for this condition can be stress, boredom, or desiring a mate. Instead of randomly preening, Lemon repeatedly plucked feathers from the same area, causing an open wound. The bird required surgery and wore a Styrofoam collar to prevent her from plucking during recovery.

When I talked to Lemon, I deduced that her preening issue resulted from stress. There had been a recent move to a new home due to divorce and although the bird loved her new apartment, and her new room, she was picking up Cheryl's stress. Lemon was also a bit lonely. I made several suggestions to Cheryl including aromatherapy. Lavender, which is used for calming, was put in a diffuser. During the consultation, Lemon told me, *It's my job to take care of my mom, Cheryl.* Apparently, the bird picked up Cheryl's anxiety about leaving Lemon alone for the entire day. Additionally, I proposed that Lemon's huge cage be moved to a room with a view and that soft jazz be played while the bird stayed alone. Lastly, I offered a homeopathic remedy, *Arsenicum album.* One drop to be put in Lemon's water would help keep her moods level. Lemon then told me her desire for banana, papaya, and kiwi. Unfortunately, the bird had no idea that these fruits are difficult to find in Chicago during the winter months. Cheryl improvised by substituting dried papaya during the winter, and Lemon is quite satisfied and appreciative. Now, Cheryl makes weekly trips to the market to purchase Lemon's other favorite foods—macaroni and cheese, chicken salad, and corn niblets.

After that, all seemed right with this Cockatoo's world until about a year later when Cheryl again called asking my help. They had moved to a new apartment in downtown Chicago and Lemon was once again preening to excess. I checked in with the Cockatoo and did not feel this was a repeat of the previous situation. I advised Cheryl to watch, but not hone in on the behavior. Be aware but don't pay too much attention to it. I added two flower essences: walnut to help with transition or change, and honeysuckle to help with the feeling of nostalgia and homesickness. Fortunately, I was correct and nothing more developed with the preening problem.

Lemon's room is painted a beautiful sky blue. Cheryl feels confident that the bird is comfortable in their new environment. Although Cheryl's work hours remain long, Lemon is released from her cage once Cheryl returns home. Together they watch television on her bed with no fear of accidents because Lemon is potty trained. The intelligent, talkative bird, with an ever-expanding vocabulary, seems content now.

⌒

I believe that if and when something is supposed to happen, it will. For a long time a dream of mine was to swim with the dolphins. The fantasy of such an adventure percolated for several years before it came to fruition. Then one day, the need to experience this phenomenon stepped to the forefront of my life. I made arrangements for a trip to the Florida Keys to visit two separate sights. However, I did wrestle with the fact that in both of these locations the dolphins are kept in a somewhat enclosed area, rather than being totally free. Never having been to either place, I decided to be open-minded about the situation. I longed to interact with the dolphins and learn from them. I felt they had secrets they wanted to share with whomever was curious enough to investigate.

When I arrived at the first facility I was immediately reassured when I saw the concern shown toward the dolphins. The dolphins swam in an enclosure off a canal where the water was murky, and the dolphins could choose whether or not they wanted to interact with humans. And visitors could not bribe the dolphins with food. Much to my delight, the dolphins were free to leave when the tide raised the water high enough to enable them to swim out. This brought me great emotional relief.

Since I was a novice, the new mask and snorkel proved awkward. We were allowed four at a time into the water with the dolphins. One male dolphin and three or four female dolphins swam with us while our activity was monitored. Respect for the dolphins was required at all times, and this swim was not to become a free for all. We were taught fundamental dolphin etiquette, and in particular not to put a hand in the blow hole.

Preoccupied, fussing with unfamiliar equipment, I did not realize that my head was underwater when I thought I heard a voice say, *You're going to hit your head!* I popped my head up out of the water to make certain it wasn't a trainer speaking. No one was there, and I wondered where in the world it had come from. Submerging myself under the water, a female dolphin appeared right next to me. Her face was next to mine, and she looked me directly in the eye. That's when I heard it again. *You are going to hit your head. You are too close to the pilings.* Looking to my right, I realized I was next to a chainlink fence that crept under the water and attached to the pilings, and indeed, I was going to hit my head. The water was so gloomy it was impossible to see clearly. Her next words, *Follow me and I will take you where you are supposed to go,* echoed in my head. Gracefully, she pulled out in front of me, and my instinct to trust her let me follow her tail fin as she guided me to the safety of the trainer's platform. The tides had somehow carried me close to the pilings and this dolphin warned me. She circled around and for the second time, looked me in the eye, and stated, *Now you're okay. You're fine.* With that said, whoosh—she was gone.

Wild thoughts raced through my head as I made my way out of the water. One of the tour leaders approached me and asked what happened. While I was experiencing this marvel, the other participants watched from the shore. I shared my experience and relayed how I actually heard the dolphin's voice in my head. Her response, like mine, was, "Wow!" The reason the dolphin warned me is because it is their nature to intervene when they feel a person needs help, whether it's physical, emotional, or spiritual. This was so gently and lovingly done, I flashed back to feelings as a toddler when my mother nudged me ever so slightly, and gently guided me back on the sidewalk. The incident was over, but the memory remains a life-long treasure.

I was still sorting through this first dolphin experience when we arrived at the next destination. This was the home of Buttons, a former show dolphin. A special program had been created for him because he loved performing his repertoire of tricks. Again, we

RANDALL HAYWARD

Lydia and dolphin

entered the water in groups of four, but the format was entirely different. Every session began with a free swim at which time we were cautioned not to reach out and grab Buttons. Given a turn to hold a stick that Buttons would jump over, we were instructed to let him interact with us. Being curious, I communicated with Buttons nonverbally, asking him how he felt doing tricks. I asked him if he was bored; if he liked having people in the water with him; and in general, how he felt about his life. His answer was clear: *This is the best possible job. I get people in the water stroking me, having fun. I get applause. I get food. I'm well-taken care of and I love coming to work every day.* What I heard in my head was confirmed by the trainers who explained that on rainy days when the program is canceled, Buttons becomes listless and loses his appetite.

One of the "don't" instructions was not to touch or stroke a dolphin specifically on the stomach, which is a sensual spot. It has been documented that dolphins are the only mammals besides humans to have sexual encounters for pleasure in addition to procreation. The pre-swim instruction covered this topic as well as explaining that the dolphins should be handled respectfully because of their high level of intelligence. During one of the early swims,

Buttons rolled up next to me, started chatting, and encouraged me to stroke him on his belly. Aware that the instructors tell visitors not to do this, Buttons reassured me, *I won't tell anybody.* Then he added, *They won't see—the water's dark enough.* So I began to stroke his belly and I could almost hear him purring, like a cat. *This feels great*, and with that said, he rolled over and as he swam away, he scrunched up his face and appeared to wink!

During the course of the week we had three swim rotations with Buttons and every swim was special. I told the trainer that Buttons sought me out and that he used healing sonar on my back. I could feel the vibration of the sonar on my back in the same area as my injury. (Sonar releases endorphins in the human brain that have a Valium-like effect.) How did the dolphin know I had sustained a back injury from a car accident? Buttons made me feel special, and he did the same for each of the people who swam with him.

My experiences with the dolphins expanded my sensibilities for many different kinds of animals and my ability to communicate with them. For the first fourteen years working as an animal communicator, I understood the animals on one particular level. However, after being with the dolphins, I began to experience greater clarity, defining more clearly the animals' messages. It is as if the dolphins peeled off my emotional layers to let more definitive impressions come through. The gift from the dolphins is a renewed self-confidence and the pleasure of communicating with all animal species.

Shilo

– Chapter Seven –

LOST PETS

*To ease another's heartache is to
forget one's pain.*

         – ABRAHAM LINCOLN

As I reach for the ringing phone, intuition tells me that the
discomfort in my stomach is not imagined. There is no dis-
cernible voice coming through the receiver, only gasping
sobs. Long before the story unfolds, I know an animal is lost.
Regardless of what kind of animal is involved the first words I can
understand through the tears are, "Help me—please help me."

Almost daily, I receive lost-pet calls from clients. Some people
rush to judge and assume that if an animal is lost, the owner must
be irresponsible and therefore the owner does not deserve to have
the pet. But even with the best of intentions accidents do happen.
The gardener did not mean to leave the gate open. The kids
thought they had closed the front door when they ran outside to
play. And sometimes the circumstances are beyond human control.
When an earthquake hits California, I always receive a rash of
calls. Life is not perfect. This is reality. This is why I am a huge pro-
ponent of identification tags on all animals. Yes, even on indoor
cats. They are not immune to venturing outside for exploration
right through an opening in a screen. It is also a wise idea to have

a flyer with the animal's picture and pertinent information ready in case your pet disappears. These flyers can be posted on trees and telephone poles around the neighborhood, and handed out in the area where your pet was last seen. When a pet is lost, time is of the essence. Any tool that could help should be initiated right away. Self-reproach and remorse serve no purpose. Guilt has never helped locate a lost animal. Action and clear thinking make the difference.

Phone calls regarding lost pets create an ocean of feelings that flow from my soul and blend with my energy. I am devastated for the calling party and I feel hurt for the lost animal. Setting all judgment aside, I focus on what has transpired, and what needs to happen immediately. Minutes matter when tracking a lost animal. Animals can travel great distances quickly. Over the years I have realized that animals travel in a counter-clockwise direction in their attempt to return home. At the same time they create a spiral shape pattern. The spiral grows longer in a north-south direction and wider in an east-west direction as the animal roams in an attempt to return home. The animal may be further thrown off course by the sheer panic of being chased by people as well as by other animals.

During these phone calls I feel tremendous frustration. There are times when I can only get people so far. An animal cannot read. So, when I step into the animals and become them, I am unable to read street signs, license plates, and mailbox numbers. I am certain the distressed owner wants to be told that her dog is on the corner of Montana Avenue and Tenth Street, but that is impossible. What I can do is say the dog is sitting next to a green dumpster behind a white fence and there are a lot of lights blinking. That is how I begin and from that point I work with the client the best I can.

Not every story has a happy ending. Not every story ends quickly within forty-eight hours. Some searches drag on for months playing havoc with human emotions. At times I have had to deal with the fact that an animal has been picked up and is being kept by a new family. In such cases clients have asked that

I help them with closure and my job then becomes assuring the distressed family that their animal companion is really all right, if that is the case. I do believe that a pet in such a situation never forgets or stops loving the first family. But life goes on, and moving on is a survival technique.

Because I believe animals are a most precious gift, and are with us on earth for such a short time, it behooves us as decent human beings to act responsibly. My love for animals is at the very foundation of who I am, and because of this conviction, I do all I can to help a client find a lost animal.

The odyssey of Whiteface certainly challenged my convictions and strengthened my belief in finding lost pets even in the face of tremendous roadblocks. This story is one of adventure and spiritual quest in every sense. It began in October with a phone call from a couple in Maryland. Formalities over, I asked the pertinent questions only to discover that Whiteface actually did not belong to Vicki and Charlie. As his name depicts, this cat did indeed have a partially white face and body with tabby markings. He was a good-size cat and thought to be about three years old.

Whiteface lived across the street from Vicki and Charlie and became a victim of the classic chronicle—the family moved and left the animal behind. Actually, the situation was a bit more complex. Whiteface, mainly an outdoor cat, had been gone for two days prior to his family's departure, thus he never understood why they vanished. He spent the first three days of the family's desertion staring in the window of his house, crying. Vicki began to put food out for the now homeless cat. Once trust was established, she intended to pick Whiteface up and adopt him. On the second day, after eating the food left for him, Whiteface disappeared. That is where the journey began.

Initial tracking began at the location where Whiteface was last seen, staring in the window of his empty house. At this point I "stepped" into his body, in a sense becoming Whiteface, and joined him as he walked down the street. When I "become" the lost animal I see things through their eyes and experience things on their visual level. The information I am able to impart to the owner is a description of places passed and other animals seen—a true "virtual reality."

What made this search extremely challenging was the fact that Whiteface was comfortable being an outdoor cat. There is a vast difference between tracking an indoor cat that has gotten out and an outdoor cat familiar with nature. The outdoor cat is unafraid of the daily goings on outside, and goes about his business as usual until something dramatic happens, perhaps being chased by a dog. The indoor cat, never having been outside, will send me better images since everything is unfamiliar and terrifying. Each impulse I receive is the result of a trauma that the lost animal experiences. This produces a strong visual and emotional imprint, so strong in fact, that it ultimately makes it easier for me to describe in detail what I am receiving.

My first attempt with Whiteface produced a clear image of a long-haired orange cat with a white chest with whom Whiteface shared several meals. I felt certain this took place at the end of their street. Vicki checked and verified that a neighbor had placed food at the location, but Whiteface had eaten and moved on.

Vicki and her husband checked with me weekly for reassurance that Whiteface was not hurt and for a "location" update. We spent a good amount of time together on the phone and I came to know and respect them. I was confident that they would persevere until Whiteface was found, joining their family of three cats and two dogs. This couple was the neighborhood watch for any animal in need, which was fortunate for the local animals. Vicki was known to have taken out a rowboat to save injured water fowl. And she thought nothing of walking on ice to rescue a stranded duck first observed from her kitchen window as she scanned the numerous channels.

It seemed that everyone in the area had a boat. Every boathouse looked the same to me and to Whiteface. Each cottage looked like the next. Each shed had a duplicate. An abundant number of waterways, both streams and canals, sparkled blue. I began to seek unusual landmarks in order to track Whiteface.

CHARLES E. TUFTS

Whiteface

One of the places Whiteface stopped had two chocolate-colored Labs who barked at him. Later the dogs' owners confirmed my Whiteface sighting, renewing hope.

Autumn was slipping into early winter, and we hoped to catch up with Whiteface soon. Food was put out to attract him, but the lure did not work. Whiteface had made an instinctual shift, becoming feral. A feral animal often eats one big meal that will satisfy him for a couple of days. The body adjusts to this way of eating, which is how nature helps wild animals survive.

For several more weeks the tracking continued. Whiteface had some marvelous adventures. There were moments when I truly believed he was on a "walkabout." (This is an Australian expression for an exploration adventure in the bush often taking a year or longer.) There were many moments when I doubted Whiteface would be found. Always, when I felt hopeless, there would be a Whiteface sighting and validation. Vicki began sending me hand-drawn maps with detailed labeling, enabling me to graph his footsteps as one would chart a ship's navigation. Photographs of various locations followed. Then it started to snow. When I placed Whiteface at a specific location, invariably, Vicki and Charlie found cat paw prints in the snow. Charlie began laying wooden planks over waterways as we anticipated Whiteface's direction, somehow trying to guide him back home.

At one point I believed we were close to victory. I knew that a cat was hiding under a porch of a vacant house, and I felt quite certain it was Whiteface. For nearly one month Vicki offered a variety of food in an attempt to coax the cat out. She used the strangest kinds of foods—strange for a cat at least. That way, when I was tracking the cat I could be sure it was Whiteface who was devouring feasts of refried beans and hard-boiled eggs. At different times, I vicariously tasted the food myself while sensing Whiteface's whereabouts.

I was positive it was our boy, but he wouldn't come out of hiding. The next step was to get permission from the owner to tear up part of the porch, which was granted. When the porch was pulled up, there was no cat, just a lot of fur. It was Whiteface's fur piled in the place where he would lay down to groom himself. After weeks of confirmation, I was extremely disheartened.

By this time, I began to ask myself, *Was this crazy?* Charlie was insistent on doing something that would be irresistible to Whiteface. Whiteface was definitely hungry and looking for food. So, in ten-degree weather, Charlie set up the barbecue and cooked salmon steaks. The aroma and the smoke filled the icy air. Vicki was bemused imagining what the neighbors were wondering, while Charlie only wanted to know if Whiteface smelled the fish. I could tell Whiteface smelled the salmon because I smelled the savory fish while I psychically tracked him nearly three thousand miles away. But still, Whiteface did not show up and we were no closer to finding him.

January was cold and lonely for the cat. Whiteface sent an image of a huge boat stored on land and an old gentleman who chased him away. Tracking became difficult. Sightings became rare. We came up with the idea of feeding stations (preset humane traps) which we called "A, B, and C." Twice a day offerings of food were left in hopes that we could determine where he was. After four months of looking we were all worn out. I had actually stopped looking and receiving, imagining it was time to be realistic.

I had followed Whiteface since October. But every time I thought about giving up I would hear from Vicki. She would tell me she was going to keep looking and she would check in with me in a month. The call would come and I would somehow "find" Whiteface and see what he was doing. This ordeal had taken a toll on all of us.

One day, unbeknownst to Vicki, Charlie called asking me to stop looking for Whiteface. He pleaded with me to tell his wife the cat was dead. He could not take anymore, and Vicki was emotionally spent. Before he hung up he quietly asked one more time, "Are you getting anything from Whiteface?" I replied that the cat was looking at an owl. He mumbled something about an owl, and then said, "What do you mean an owl?" He hung up the phone and twenty minutes later called back yelling that someone had put a plastic owl in the tree next to the cat's feeding station.

Two days later Vicki called me, unaware of the recent conversation I had with Charlie. Innocently, I said that Whiteface was looking at a plastic owl on the ground. As predicted, Vicki called me back reporting that a plastic owl lay on the ground near a feeding station.

Spring had brought with it warm weather and several people had spotted Whiteface, worn thin from the winter. Hopeful again, we discussed preparations for Whiteface's capture, truly convinced we would get him. On their front porch, Charlie built a cage as a temporary enclosure. Sure enough, one June day Vicki called me and said through her tears, "We've got him!" Whiteface ended up on the front porch of his old house, which still remained vacant. Vicki tiptoed softly toward him and picked him up. Whiteface was too tired to fight. He spent two weeks in the temporary isolation cage until he was once again comfortable being handled by people.

A few months later I was in Maryland attending a dog show and I had the opportunity to spend an evening with these special people. We met for dinner and returned to Vicki and Charlie's home so I could meet Whiteface in person. He came over to me immediately and sent me a message, loud and clear. *Oh, you're the one who was looking for me!* Today Whiteface seems to have recovered from this eight-month ordeal. He is now part of a loving family. Undoubtedly, Whiteface has many a tale to tell and has used several of his nine lives.

In contrast to Whiteface and the numerous strikes against him, many lost pets come from safe, loving, and protected homes where circumstance just happens to make the great escape possible. Such was the saga of Boy George, an Abyssinian show cat owned by one of my roommates, Rainy. After returning to California with an assortment of animals, I rented a small house with three people. My career as an animal communicator was in its infancy and we all helped each other with necessary animal care when travel plans arose. On this particular occasion, I was back east visiting my family when I received a call from Rainy. She was hysterical and it was difficult to get the details, but easy to feel her panic and know that Boy George was gone. Apparently, to cool off the house on a warm summer evening, a window had been opened, and the cat slipped through a hole in the screen.

The house was in a rural area that was refuge to wild dog packs, coyotes, hawks, and owls. George, as he was known, had no street smarts and had never been outside without the protection of a carrier or in a cat harness. To make matters worse, since he lived with our house dogs, George had no reason to fear canines; therefore, the wild dogs would be of no particular concern to him. So at midnight with three thousand miles between us, Rainy held a cellular phone to her ear with one hand and a flashlight in the other as we began to track George.

Rainy called out the cat's name and waited a few seconds while I picked up George's whereabouts. When I was convinced the cat heard her, I pinpointed the location and described it. Repeatedly, she would approach the site just in time to hear her cat scurry away. George was having a good time playing hide and seek, and this adventure was filled with excitement. George was in no hurry to return home. He actually was glad, or at least flattered, that his owner was upset.

For three days I followed George, asking Rainy to look in a variety of different locations. After checking each spot, she phoned back, reporting his latest whereabouts. The last day I felt George saunter to the end of the block and cross the street. I saw him staring at a large metal building. Following my mental map, Rainy discovered an abandoned Quonset hut perched on pilings. By this time, George was unhappy and lost.

Arriving just in time to see George run underneath the structure, she thought the chase was over. However, cajoling him out became a task more difficult than finding him. The dark, dank crawl space was not only tiny, but inhabited by spiders and snakes. Rainy was terrified of both, but for the love of her animal, she slid under the hut, dragging herself through the dirt, calling his name and begging him to appear. This tactic produced no results. A jar of baby food was the magic needed to coax George into daylight. Baby food was a special treat saved solely for cat shows. Tapping the lid and enticing him with the aroma of "Gerber's Chicken" mixed with encouraging words, he meowed. As he moved closer, Rainy managed to grab him. There was no reason to get angry, besides poor George was terrorized.

Once home, George stayed in Rainy's bedroom for days. He sat in the window and stared, but he never acted as though he desired to venture out. He had learned his lesson. When I got home, I asked him, "George, why?" He responded, *I wanted to see the birds and the butterflies.* Perhaps this cat's name should have been "Curious George."

An overwhelming majority of lost pets are dogs and cats. Phone calls regarding missing snakes are few and far between, but they do occur. Debbie called asking help in locating her children's pet Boa Constrictor, Bruce. He measured somewhere between three and four feet long. He had pushed the lid off his tank, and Debbie was certain he was investigating the house. I had once helped her horse, so she felt confident that I could find the snake. Beginning with routine questions of geographic location and the animal's name, I quietly concentrated on Bruce, determined to find where he might have gone. I thought for a minute and said,

"He is up underneath metal coils. He is in coils, like a mattress or a chair. All I see are coils and he is in there."

A bewildered Debbie moaned that Bruce's tank was located in her son's bedroom and that she had torn apart her son's bedroom to no avail. Again, I told her, "All I can tell you is what I feel and what I see. He is in coils. It may not be a mattress. It maybe something else, but it has coils."

Debbie's son was beginning to worry that Bruce might have run away. He desperately needed to know if Bruce was upset about being kept in a tank. Reassuring her the answer was "no" to both of those questions, I added that the snake noticed an opening and went for a hike. Debbie confessed that her son often allowed Bruce to cruise around his room while he did homework. However, this disappearing act took place while the family was at a soccer match, and the house was quiet.

About an hour passed when an elated Debbie called back to tell me that Bruce had been found. "Where?" I asked. "Inside the coils of the recliner!" she replied. When success comes this quickly, I not only feel elated but extremely fortunate. It's like tying the last piece of ribbon around a gift.

Shilo's story took a different road. Many times the possibility of a happy ending with a lost animal appears bleak. However, my experience with Shilo reinforced my belief that animals, like people, do have guardian angels. In 1995 Fumi telephoned asking for help in finding Shilo, a wolf-hybrid. We began the search during the Thanksgiving holiday. At the same time, I learned the sad story of Shilo's life.

At six weeks of age, when young pups are playing and nuzzling with mom and siblings, Shilo was given to her only owner, a man who attached her to the end of a chain. About eighty percent wolf, this was Shilo's life until she was four years old. At that time her owner, planning to move out of state, decided to let her go free. As bizarre as it sounds, the owner was encouraged to leave Shilo behind, chained, assured that someone knowledge-able would care for her. Some compassionate animal lovers had been painfully aware of Shilo's miserable life. (Shilo was about thirty pounds underweight and abused.) So, they came up with a rescue plan that involved convincing the owner to leave Shilo. He agreed.

Within minutes of the owner's departure, the preplanned rescue began. Fumi, having participated in wolf-hybrid rescue, was called to supervise the event. Four people filled with love and assisted by a vet tech approached the wolf. Aware that Shilo would be fearful of men, Fumi insisted on talking to the animal solo. She took her time, first introducing herself and then talking Shilo through each step as they proceeded. Fumi spoke to Shilo as the tech injected a tranquilizer into Shilo's thigh to calm her down. However, the dog tranquilizer they used was ineffective on Shilo because this wolf-hybrid is predominantly wolf. Fortunately, Shilo immediately trusted Fumi, who used positive, loving words mixed with high-pitched sounds that comforted the wolf. Shilo then allowed this strange woman, turned friend, to touch behind her ears and then rub her stomach.

When Shilo was as relaxed as possible, they cut the chain. The metal links of Shilo's bondage had been wrapped around a tree about two inches from its base and had been there so long that it cut a deep groove into the tree trunk from Shilo's four years of confinement. Looking at the tree, Fumi could only wonder what this animal had endured at the end of that twenty-foot chain. It had taken nearly two hours to free her. Fumi slipped a leash and collar over Shilo's head and walked her to the car. Fumi asked Shilo to get in and the wolf willingly obeyed. Shilo was taken to a foster home to live with Addie, one of her rescuers.

Thanksgiving Day was festive as Addie and Shilo joined Fumi and her family. The wolf joyfully ran around the heavily wooded, fenced yard. On the way home Addie had car trouble and she and Shilo walked to a nearby shopping center to call for help. Unfortunately, the phone was inside the store and Shilo was tied to a post. Two minutes later when Addie returned, she found Shilo missing. Immediately, Addie called Fumi and after hours of searching with no leads they returned to their respective homes. Unable to sleep during the night, Fumi sat in the kitchen. In her restlessness, she picked up a newsletter from a local pet supply store and read about a visit from an animal psychic. Fumi was desperate and she figured it was worth a try. Fumi called me as soon as the sun came up Friday.

Unfamiliar with the area, I had to use a map. Fumi pinpointed the exact spot from which Shilo disappeared. Picking up Shilo's energy, I honed in on a location directly northwest, somewhere between twenty and twenty-five minutes away by car. I also visualized two German Shepherds at this destination.

Saturday morning, Fumi and Addie headed out, following my directions and arrived at the County Animal Shelter. When they entered the shelter they noticed two German Shepherds. Holding a photo of Shilo, Fumi approached an animal control officer, who reacted angrily. He not only confessed to having seen Shilo the day before, but admitted he shot her with a tranquilizer dart and conceded she did not go down. The two women and the animal control officer left the shelter and went to the woods where Shilo was last seen. They hiked the trails calling for Shilo. Suddenly, without a sound, Shilo emerged, the dart hanging from her dragging leg. The wolf timidly approached Fumi and licked her face. Fumi held Shilo tightly between her legs, and turned the wolf's face away from the animal control officer as he removed the dart. It was not known at that time, but Shilo had sustained a hairline fracture from the dart's impact. When Fumi took Shilo home, the wolf spotted Fumi's husband and still fearful of men, she panicked. Shilo ran causing the injured leg to break completely.

The vet's suggestion was to euthanize Shilo, concerned about the anesthetic risk and the prolonged recovery time. Fumi was committed to Shilo, and euthanasia was not an option. The wolf was immediately taken to a specialist for a second opinion. Seven screws and one plate later, covered by a solid cast, Shilo was on the road to recovery. Healing took longer than expected. Since a wolf will pace instinctively and pacing impedes healing, Shilo had to remain in a confined area with twenty-four hour care. While Shilo recovered and slept on the floor, her guardian angel, Fumi, slept on a sofa right next to her. Their relationship continues to grow.

Thankfully, the majority of lost pet narratives are not quite as dramatic as Shilo's, and most animals do not suffer the pain and indignity she endured. Living through the search for a missing animal is traumatic and stressful for every owner but each story has its own flavor, and each one is compelling.

I was called to help locate a dog who vanished on a forty-acre ranch in Texas. Other than expanses of flat grass, there was nothing on this land except for a tall telephone pole topped with a red search light. The red beam was a warning for airplane navigation, since a sound tower stood nearby. Using the red light as a guide, I was able to identify the dog's location. This taught me to be aware of unusual landmarks, which proved to be an invaluable lesson. For example, if a frightened animal is hiding under a car, the view seen looking up at the underside of the car will be the same from one car to the next. And, if an animal is hiding under a dumpster, the view looking up at the underside of one dumpster will be the same as any other. Conscious of such similarities, I am able to clarify the confusion by looking for unusual details.

Early in my career I assisted in a search for an exotic parrot when the cage door was accidentally opened. The bird managed to fly out of the house through an open window while the parrot's mate stayed safely in their shared cage. Trying to track the parrot was impossible since he was flying over a condominium development where all the houses looked the same. The problem was resolved when the female bird, still in her cage, was placed outside on the ground adjacent to an empty cage. As soon as the free bird heard his mate calling, he landed on top of the cage and it was possible to catch him.

Andy was the mule that almost ran away. In the midst of a group session, having just finished a consultation for a seventy-year old gentleman who trained mules, I turned and moved on to my next client. Andy had been tied to a trailer so the sound of his clop—clop—clop was hard to ignore. This mule had untied himself. With his halter on and lead rope trailing behind, he headed down a main road toward the local highway. Not knowing what else to do I yelled, "Andy, stand still!" The mule screeched to a halt and stood still in the middle of the road saying, *Yup, I'm standing still—Now what do you want?* Creeping up next to him, while verbally reminding him to stand still, I picked up the lead rope and we headed back. The elderly man stood, wide-eyed in disbelief, and uttered, "Lady, in seventy years I ain't seen anything like that!"

Judd was a Greyhound racing dog who had been rescued after he was discarded by owners only interested in a winning dog. He had slipped out of his collar and leash while on a walk with his new owner. Although Judd had been in this loving home for two months, he had panicked and bolted. During a consultation, I got a clear picture from Judd in a drainage ditch. The feeling that accompanied the image was Judd's need for a place to den and figure his way out of this dilemma. The following day Judd sent me a picture of a single picnic table, not at a park, but one lone table. His owners recognized this landmark, which was near their condo and they realized Judd was trying to find his way home. The third day I felt that Judd had moved further along and was in a place made of concrete that had a grate. That night while walking through the carport, his owners heard Judd bark. Somehow, Judd had managed to maneuver himself through the drainage tunnel, and followed this path to the point where it went under the carport. Shining a light down the grate confirmed that it definitely was their dog. It took an animal lover from the parks department, to complete this rescue.

A kind woman, Catherine, called me about a dog she had found. She wanted desperately to know where the dog had come from. I explained to her that without his name and with the geographical distance separating us, I needed a photo of the dog. That way, I could be certain that I was tuning into the dog's frequency. A photo of a melancholy Basset Hound arrived and the consultation began with Catherine providing what background she had.

With no collar or tags, the dog had roamed her neighborhood for two weeks. All sorts of people chased him as he avoided capture.

Then one day he ran to Catherine, stood still until she put her grocery bags down, and attempted to jump up into her arms. Catherine knew the dog was trying to tell her something but she was uncertain of the message. I felt she had a Basset Hound somewhere in her past, and there lay the connection. My sense was that the dog was looking for someone to help him, and wanted to be with a person who knew and understood his breed. I also added that the dog greeted Catherine as a long-lost friend. There was silence. Stunned, Catherine explained to me that she had a Basset Hound as a child. Now she chose to adopt this dog, or perhaps, this dog chose her.

When I took this Basset back in time, he showed me his family moving. When they departed, he followed their car, running up the road for as many miles as he could, until the car vanished. Left behind, he began looking for help and he waited for somebody with whom he could connect. Obviously, I could not verify this scenario. In my opinion, the Basset selected Catherine, and this was not an accident. The dog healed her heart and filled the void left by the childhood animal companion she still missed. And in turn, Catherine helped the Basset heal and recover from the abuse of being a throw-away pet.

Most of the clients I help with lost pets I do not know. I rarely have the opportunity to help a friend locate a lost animal. When the opportunity presented itself, as it did with my friend Randy, I was eager to help. Randy was visiting a friend whose dog Rocky, a Miniature Doberman Pinscher, zipped out the door wearing a collar with tags. They chased Rocky up the block, and then lost his trail as he turned the corner. Although I was called within two hours, the sun had set and it was dark. I was certain that Rocky could see floodlights hitting the side of a building with ivy around it. Then I added that the wall was slate blue. As an afterthought I mentioned, "Rocky showed me a white wrought-iron fence." That was the clincher. Confident that he knew the exact location, Randy ran out and twenty minutes later Rocky was back home. Randy found the dog in the setting I pictured.

The stress and excitement were too much for Pippen, a gray

and orange tabby who watched his owner, Wendy, pack moving boxes. Pippen's world was being turned upside down. Cartons were everywhere. When the door opened Pippen slipped out. Frantically, Wendy posted flyers and offered reward money. Wendy and her mother took turns looking for the cat and calling his name as they wandered the neighborhood. By the time they contacted me they were both distraught and exhausted. I felt that Pippen was within twenty feet of their front steps. Without a doubt he heard them screaming his name. Assuming he was in trouble because of their tone of voice, Pippen was too frightened to return. My suggestion was to sit quietly on the steps and in a soft voice talk to Pippen and call his name. Wendy tried this and within thirty minutes he meowed and appeared.

Not every animal who vanishes is lost. This story has a unique twist because I was asked to help after the missing dog had been reunited with his owner. Smith, an American Staffordshire Terrier, disappeared without a trace from what might be considered the safest place of all. Smith was stolen and taken from his crate at a dog show. His crate was set in the shade along side many other crated dogs, while Diana, his owner, walked to the ring to check the schedule. A professionally dressed man appearing to be a handler, opened the door to the carrier and walked off with Smith on a show lead.

Since I was lecturing out of town, my secretary spoke with Diana advising her that she must remain as calm and positive as possible. Because Smith would be able to pick up her emotions, it was important that she stay composed. Diana did not panic.

The dog show had been held on a high school campus, and security immediately called the police. They used a Blood Hound who picked up Smith's scent and followed the scent to a red painted curb, a fire zone, where he then lost the scent. Witnesses recognized Smith's picture and described a man who put the dog in a white van. Two and one-half days later, Smith was seen running around a college campus across town. He finally settled down to rest under a group of eucalyptus trees. Diana had placed flyers all over the vicinity and a student recognized Smith's picture from the flyer and called police. Diana picked Smith up at the police station. He was exhausted from the ordeal and slept for hours.

Diana wanted me to find out exactly what happened from Smith's perspective and if the dog was still interested in being shown. A few days later, when Smith had relaxed, I communicated with him. Knowing none of the details, I described a dark-haired man, wearing a beige tweed jacket, show lead in hand, take Smith from his crate. Smith thought the man was a handler who was walking him to his "mom" ringside. When Smith realized he was being led away from the ring, he was confused. (Show dogs are trained to be obedient and they are often led to the ring by different handlers who help each other out.)

From Smith's perspective, I saw a white van and felt him being pushed into a crate. There were two other crated dogs in the van, one of whom told Smith, *You are my next battle.* It was at this point Smith realized he was in trouble, for the dog intended to fight him. When the man stopped for gas, he gave the dogs water, and accidentally left the latch on Smith's crate partially open. At the next stop, I saw Smith break out of the crate, pushing the wire door with his head. (He pushed so hard when escaping that the impression at the wire door was still visible on his head hours later when reunited with Diana.) He headed for the big open green of the college campus. I saw him near a tall building sitting under a clump of eucalyptus trees. Diana said the tall building was the library and near it was a cluster of eucalyptus trees—the exact spot where Smith was found.

Smith is back on the show circuit and he seems genuinely happy. As Diana requested, I spoke to him and Smith no longer goes willingly with anyone other than his owner unless he has a verbal okay from Diana.

Sadly there are animals who are stolen, and in some cases kept when found, even though the people know who the pet belongs to. They will throw away the tag, keep the animal, and continue to call the pet by its original name. How can people rationalize that this is acceptable?

Because all humans do not respect animals as individual living beings, this behavior will continue. And those of us who truly love our animal companions as family members will have to be careful in watching over our animals.

My animals are precious to me and as their caretaker I take every precaution to protect them. All of my animals are trained to come when they are called. The cats are trained with treats. Before I leave home I make certain that I see each animal. If they are hidden or sleeping somewhere, I call them and they usually peek their head out and show me where they are. I double check all screens and the doors as well. Both canines and felines wear tags on their collars. Off my property they are on leash. These procedures give me peace of mind.

If you are faced with the agony of losing a pet, remember: **Lost animals move in a counter-clockwise direction and spiral out in an ever widening circle. When an animal travels, he or she most likely will do so at first light or at dusk.**

The more people who can be on the alert, the better. Ask mail carriers, UPS drivers, neighbors, and kids on bikes to be on the lookout. Be sure to let people know there is a reward involved. Just in case, be prepared with flyers and a good photo. File it away and hope that "lost" flyer will never be used.

Hunyak

– Chapter Eight –

ANIMALS IN SPIRIT

*Grief differs even as emotional makeup differs
from individual to individual.*
– THE REVEREND M. GREGORY RICHARDS

Only in recent years has the loss of a beloved animal been taken seriously. As the relationship between animal and human is recognized and respected, the enormous emotion over the death of an animal loss is acknowledged. The attitude that "it is only an animal" is slowly being replaced with grief counseling centers and support groups for those whose animal companions have died. Even pet loss hot lines are becoming more common. The University of California at Davis, School of Veterinary Medicine, has such a hot line.

The firsthand knowledge gained from living through each personal loss contributes to our wholeness as human beings. My experience in dealing with the loss of my first dog, Ginger, had a tremendous impact on me as a child and is directly responsible for the way in which I counsel my clients today. As an adult, I felt it was my obligation to make the difficult and final decision to euthanize my beloved Hunyak. My commitment to him was as powerful as his devotion to me and it became my duty to recognize when it was time to let him go. Having lived through events such as these with loving support from family and friends, I have learned how to help people who reach out to me in their time of need.

With the proliferation of interest in animal- and pet-related issues, the opportunity for my appearances on television programs has increased dramatically. I was a guest on an emotional segment of "The Leeza Show," dealing with divorcing couples fighting over their dogs. A young man in the audience, obviously perplexed by the passion displayed by the battling couples, raised his hand to comment. Thinking that the situation was ridiculous, he asked why one of the spouses did not go out and simply get another dog. There was a collective gasp from the crowd.

To myself, I thought, *Lydia, he doesn't have a clue—proceed with caution.* In a voice, gentle and sincere, I replied, "Maybe a pet hasn't touched your life yet. Though, once that happens, it really changes your life." It was difficult to clear my head of what transpired. After the taping, I thought about that exchange for a long time, ruminating on the young man's comment about just getting another dog. He had never been touched by a special animal and the unconditional love, the loyalty, the wet kisses, and the soft paw that can be a part of this relationship. He also was missing out on having to say good-bye when a human and pet become separated by death.

Oftentimes, animal lovers can grieve more deeply for a companion animal than for a person. It is difficult to prepare for the strong feelings and reactions over the loss of a pet. Animals have told me their bodies are merely "spacesuits" and once free of this protective garb, they play again as puppies with no ailments or pain. ("Spacesuit" is my interpretation of what the animals show me to be their "physical package" versus their "spiritual package.")

Ginger, my childhood Collie, was basically a healthy dog most of her life and did not need the vet for anything more serious than inoculations. When Ginger became ill it was apparent that she was really in trouble. Her symptoms were loss of appetite, panting, and fever. I recall my father and I taking her to the vet. As a six-year old listening to the adult conversation, I remember the vet saying Ginger needed fluids and that it was "serious." Ginger would need surgery, and we would pick her up the following day. It was a long restless night at home without her, but I had said good-bye to Ginger and reassured her that we would be back the next day.

The following morning the whole family went to pick up Ginger and bring her home. But instead of Ginger, we were handed her leash and collar accompanied by a sincere apology. Ginger had passed away in the middle of the night. My parents, brother, and I stood in the waiting room stunned, devastated, unable to move—unable to comprehend. No one called our home to inform us. I can still see the vet holding a limp collar and leash, and saying those haunting words "in the middle of the night." The vet looked old with his shock of white hair as he said, "I'm sorry." I believe he was, but no additional support was offered, and we left, our hearts broken.

In addition to Ginger's death, one other situation painted an indelible impression upon me and the importance of grieving. While working at a veterinary hospital shortly after relocating to California, a woman carried a cat into the clinic. The animal had been hit by a car and was nearly dead on arrival. The woman's son, perhaps five years old, was crying and frightened. To placate him, she said, "Don't worry honey, we'll just go out and get another one." I was stupefied by how the mother chose not to address the child's grief. The opportunity to talk to her son about death and strengthen his understanding of death evaporated in that moment. Her decision to opt for a quick fix, an instant repair, sent a clear message that this animal was disposable, and easily replaceable. Upon reflection, I can only hope that this woman's behavior and her suggestion to replace the animal were made in her own moment of grief and her desire to shield her child from pain.

What I have learned over the years is that one animal can *never* replace another. Each animal is as unique and individual as a human being. Every animal in a litter is one of a kind. I have also observed that a division of people exists—those who treat animals as property, and those who treat animals as family members with love and respect. Unfortunately, there are numerous animals who fall into the category of "throw-away animals."

An orange tabby was one such animal. A compassionate woman on her way to work, found this seriously hurt, stray cat wandering down the street. She brought the cat to the animal hospital where I was employed as a vet tech. The cat was the victim of a hit-and-run incident. When the stray cat was handed to me, I called her Pumpkin.

As I held Pumpkin, a chill passed through me because of her uncanny resemblance to Jane, my orange feline who had died nearly a year before. Pumpkin's jaw was broken and her face had been partially crushed. The cat had great difficulty breathing. I heard every breath and gurgle, but clearly perceived her request, *I need a drink of water.* She accepted individual droplets of water, although her tongue had been split. Once we made Pumpkin as comfortable as possible, humanitarian efforts to save her were discussed realistically. As the afternoon wore on I received strong statements from this brave orange cat, *Let me go. I don't even want to be around.* I questioned her, *Who is your family?* Pumpkin never vacillated, repeating over and over, *I'm a stray cat. Nobody really wants me. I don't want to go through this. I am ready to go.*

So certain about her messages, and acutely aware of the painful reconstructive surgery ahead, I honored Pumpkin's wishes and approached the vet. He agreed that euthanasia was appropriate. The only question posed by the vet was whether I was certain about holding the cat as she was put to sleep. I was certain. Within seconds, Pumpkin left her body. And as I held Pumpkin's physical body, I could feel her spirit body rubbing against my legs. Released from her body, moments after being euthanized, Pumpkin's image appeared in front of me like a hologram. And I could see that her body looked whole and healthy. Her jaw was in alignment and she was able to breath. I heard her say, *Thank you.* Then the hologram faded, but the lesson remained. This was the first time I experienced an animal spirit leave its physical body—a damaged physical body—and appear whole. My experience tells me that the precise reason an animal asks to be released is because the body no longer functions, but the spirit continues.

⌇

Making the final decision whether or not to euthanize a pet is one of the most difficult and painful choices pet owners are called upon to make. This decision can be wrought with conflicting feelings of guilt and relief. Clients have often told me that the decision to euthanize a companion pet has often been referred to as "the most important decision of my life." Gary Kowalski, author of *Goodbye Friend*, a book about pet lovers dealing with the loss of an animal, writes:

> *Perhaps our animals can guide us as well as console us at such times. For if most organisms have an innate survival instinct that drives them to cling to life against all odds, many also seem to possess an inborn sense that tells them when the time has come to let go and bow to the inevitable.*

When people are faced with this decision, I offer the perspective that they are choosing to set the animal free. I believe that acknowledging an animal is ready to go is the ultimate act of loving unselfishness on the part of an owner. Granted, this is not a decision that should be made quickly, or based solely on the owner's convenience. However, I have learned from the animals that there are times when they want to be euthanized.

The grief process ebbs and flows and may be speckled with flashes of relief, which cause people to wonder, "How dare I feel relief?" Then they feel guilty about feeling relief. I believe that a feeling of relief also comes from the animal, who is saying, *I know I am going to be whole when I am free of my body. I know the leg that is missing is going to be there. I know the cancer in my stomach will be gone. I know the pain I am feeling will be no more. And once you release me I can run again!*

These are my beliefs, which have unfolded over many years of working with animals. Yet, I understand that this can be an impossible stretch for many. However, I am an advocate of an open mind and the right to be a skeptic. But before I continue with other stories of animal spirits, it is necessary to explain my beliefs concerning how animals "cross over."

For years there have been stories about humans having near-death experiences or actually dying, and then coming back to tell about the event. There seems to be a shared commonality among those who lived through this phenomenon. They see a bright light and are met by a familiar and loving family member or friend. From what I have witnessed in the animal kingdom it is not that different from what humans have described. Although validation of this experience is more difficult with animals, once again, I have to trust my inner voice.

When an animal is severely ill, he or she may reach the point of teetering on the threshold of crossing over. Animals in this situation will visualize to me another animal—perhaps an animal friend, or an animal they have lived with, or even possibly an animal stranger they have never met. When the time comes to die, I am convinced animals never cross over alone. I also believe that animals like humans have spirit guides or guardian angels. My conviction is based on the many animal messengers (animals themselves have visualized other animals) that I have described to human clients in addition to the personal experiences I have had. I have seen animals in a "hologram" state. I have also felt the physical sensation of a nose bob from a dog, or a cat's tail rubbing against my leg immediately after they have died. Clients also have told me rather incredible spiritual stories of animal companions dying and their spirits making themselves known.

My acceptance of animal messengers evolved over a period of time, dating back to my training days. Early on the seeds were planted and with each remarkable story the roots of this phenomenon strengthened and I evolved from a skeptic to believer. My education of animals in spirit and animal messengers began with the passing of Baby, who was the last of five generations of Shih

Tzus owned by Jean, a devoted dog owner. When Baby was fourteen years old, and quite ill, Jean realized her beloved animal companion needed to be euthanized. Jean worried that her precious dog would meet death alone, which left her feeling extremely uncomfortable. Jean wanted to be with Baby at this juncture and made the decision to hold her as she was put to sleep.

After confirming the details with Baby's vet, an appointment time was scheduled for this sad event. As Jean left her house, she intuitively grabbed her camera. When the vet gave the dog the injection, Jean held Baby in her arms. Once Baby stopped breathing, the vet listened with a stethoscope and pronounced the dog dead. Jean asked for a few minutes alone to say a private good-bye. The vet left the room, closing the door. Without knowing why, Jean took a photograph of Baby.

Several days later Jean picked up her photos, eager to see the last memory of her beloved dog. Expecting to pay the bill, and be on her way, she was surprised to find her photos had been pulled. She was quite upset to hear that something was wrong with her pictures. Apparently, there were unusual images in the photo, "ghostlike" in the words of the salesclerk. Jean opened the envelope and leaned against the counter as she gasped, "Oh, my God!" There in the photo, behind Baby, were images of all four of her dogs—the four who had already passed on. The dogs had come back as a group, not just one messenger, but all four, to help Baby cross over.

Animals continually report incredible information to me. A new client, Joy, called with questions about euthanizing Smokey, her ill sixteen-year old cat. The decision overwhelmed Joy, who felt the cat was nearly ready to be released. Joy wanted confirmation from me. She also wanted to know if I believed that an animal guardian would help her loving companion cross over—and who that angel might be. After chatting for awhile, I told Joy I agreed with her decision. Smokey was ready to be set free. Curious, I asked her where she would have encountered a Siberian Tiger because Smokey had visualized such an animal as his guardian angel. Joy gasped, and when she regained composure, told me the story of how, as a young woman traveling in India, she had met such a tiger in the wild. From this one incident, she grew to love tigers and her home was filled with Siberian Tiger artifacts. It made perfect sense to her and gave her peace of mind.

Pet owners tell of seeing out of the corner of an eye their departed animal or they see the deceased pet in dreams. Others have noticed an impression on the bed, left in the favorite spot where the deceased animal used to rest. Many of these incidents are reported by people who have no other living animal in the home, and they wonder what else is possible from an animal who has entered the spirit world.

Is it wishful thinking or is it really the animal returning to check on the grieving owner? Certainly, my feelings would not satisfy the scientific mind. However, I truly believe that although the animal no longer carries his or her physical body, all the love remains. It is the physical body we humans yearn to hug and touch because we live in our bodies in a physical world. But if we can call on the freedom of belief we had as children and imagine what it would be like to have only that animal's spirit around, all kinds of possibilities unfold.

When the mind is open, the animal's energy—a heart memory— can come into our space. The only difference is that there is a "veil" between us, and although we may not see them in full form as we did when they were alive, we can still experience our animals through our senses. For instance, one of my clients had a dog who died, and two days later experienced his presence. Her dog, while alive, loved to roll in the garden in the fresh compost, which had a strong pungent odor. The smell was very distinct, and became a fond part of the owner and dog's memories together. Two days after the dog died, and the carpets had been cleaned, the woman was sitting in her living room reading the newspaper. It was the middle of winter and the windows were closed. Suddenly, that familiar scent wafted through the air and she knew it was her beloved dog. She later told me, "This was my first realization that there is something after this life. Knowing my dog is still out there in spirit gives me great peace."

Other clients have told me about seeing outlines of their pets' bodies, or hearing them bark, and feeling them lick their hands, or just having some strong sense of the animal companions being present. I believe without a doubt that the love and the cellular memories ingrained within each of us make it possible for our animal companions to remain after they have died. This theory brings comfort and relief to many.

~

In my work, I am acutely aware whether or not animals are imparting knowledge. Not every orange cat is meant to be an instructor, but Pumpkin bestowed a great lesson and another orange cat, Jane, taught me as well. While living and working at the stable in New Jersey, I found Jane. Well, actually, she found me. This is often the case. The cat population frequently runs rampant in a barn environment and this stable was no exception. Jane was from a litter of five kittens. I had no intention of owning a cat, and for the longest time Jane had no name and was simply called the "orange kitten." One day I saw her tiny orange body walking toward me from the far end of the barn. She had something in her mouth, and I thought, *She has a twig in her mouth. How sweet, she's bringing me a gift.* As she approached I realized the gift was moving. The twig was a baby snake, still very much alive. Gentle Jane never hurt the snake, she was merely giving me a present. This was the moment that clinched my decision to adopt her.

Spaying and neutering the cats halted the barn's feline population, but an abundance of felines remained. One day after returning from a horse show, I noticed that no cats were around. After a brief search, I asked a barn hand where the cats were. Very matter of factly he responded that they were gone forever. Pressing him for details, I learned that a man had carried twenty cats away in burlap bags. Jane was among them. She was sent to a ranch down the road where she would hunt mice. Immediately I went to the rancher to get Jane back. However, the rancher insisted on a trade, one good hunter for another. I promised to find such an animal even if I had to conjure one up. I begged him, in the meanwhile, to keep Jane safe. The man definitely thought I was crazy. Bewildered and annoyed by my concern, he snapped, "It's just a cat!"

Two cats still remained at the barn, too agile and smart to be caught. I approached the cats very slowly, talking to them and picturing plump mice. The wildest cat, who did not let anybody touch him, allowed me to pick him up. As I drove him to his new home at the ranch, he calmly sat beside me. The trade was made and Jane became a house cat from that day forth. Officially part of my family, Jane moved with me from East Coast to West Coast and made the transition easily. Jane and I were special companions.

I had the opportunity to spend a week with a veterinarian in Minnesota, who was doing some interesting work with holistic medicine and the use of aloe vera as an internal cleanser and for external healing. Convinced that his work was important, I shelved the nagging feeling about traveling and packed. My animals were safe, cared for by Rolf, my roommate. The vet was a wealth of knowledge and like a sponge, I soaked up every word he uttered.

Midweek, an orange cat was brought in for boarding. Her resemblance to Jane was unsettling. The animal was not ill, but for some reason her presence caused me to become extremely upset. The uncomfortable feeling was validated the moment our eyes met. The cat communicated, *I am a messenger—Jane is not alive anymore.* These were words I heard in my head, but I answered verbally, "What?" Then I thought, this is ridiculous. Jane is healthy. She was inoculated against anything that could conceivably hurt her and she was safe at home. I called home anyway, and because of the time difference there was no answer. Several hours elapsed before I talked with Rolf on the phone. I blurted out my concerns. Convincingly, he responded, "Let me look for her. I just walked in the house. I'll call you back. I'm sure she's okay." I waited. With each passing minute the potential that something was wrong grew. Fifteen minutes later the call came. Jane had died, curled up in her favorite spot underneath a bathroom cabinet on a towel kept there for her. At first Rolf thought she was sleeping because she was still warm to the touch. Later it was determined that Jane died from a heart attack.

At first, I could not comprehend the meaning behind this message. Usually the messenger is an animal who has already crossed over. This was the first and only time a live animal acted as a courier to me. Jane and her messenger could have been identical twins by their solid orange marmalade coloring and the three black dots on the nose. In addition, I later learned that females of this type of coloring are rare. Jane was only three years old and I had no idea her life was close to ending. I was forced to accept it was her time to cross over. Many of my clients have cried to me that they should have known. But sometimes we are not aware that it is the animal's time to leave.

Thirty percent of my business is counseling clients who are faced with decisions about euthanizing their pet and they question *when* is the right time. Each case is personal but a common thread connects them all. In such a heartbreaking situation, when we feel as though our back is up against the wall and we do not have a choice—that is the moment the animal is saying, *Release me from this physical body. I am ready to go.* That is the request. This has been my experience with my own animals. When animals who are ready to be released from their bodies arrive at the hospital, they may need only one-tenth the dose of Euthanol calculated for their weight. Animals prepared to cross over quickly

MICHAEL PARAS

Hunyak and Lydia

only require a little bit of help. People ask me, "Why don't all animals just cross over in their sleep? It would make it much easier for us. We wouldn't have to make that choice." My response is that there are lessons the animal is still teaching us to the end.

When my dog Hunyak was alive he accompanied me almost everywhere. We were traveling companions. On one particular trip we were driving from our home in California to Oregon. It was a cold winter evening and total darkness had fallen. My watch read close to seven o'clock, which meant it was time for Hunyak's rest stop. As I began looking for a place to pull over, he started whining. Checking the rear-view mirror, I could see Hunyak's head cocked, and his ears up. Undoubtedly, he was agitated, but not because he needed the rest stop. He continued to whine. Then his hair stood up. Hunyak acted as if someone was in the van with us, but who? We were alone, at least to my knowledge. As I approached the turnoff, I glanced to my right and was surprised to see a "shadow image" of Lucy, my friend's black Lab. The image was sitting next to me. A moment later, the image disappeared. Perplexed, I stopped and calmly tried to make sense of the now-faded image.

Lucy belongs to my friend Jo, who lives in Illinois, and I knew all of her animals well. "Seeing" Lucy made no sense, because Jo had not called me to say the dog was sick. Feeling uneasy about the apparition, I called home to check in. There was a message from Jo explaining that Lucy was critically ill and she was asking whether the dog should be put to sleep. Immediately, I called Jo in Illinois. The phone rang and rang. Checking my watch, I decided to call again in half an hour. When I got back in the van, Hunyak seemed relaxed. But when I started exiting the rest area, I sensed Lucy's presence again. Then I heard, *I'm fine now. You don't have to worry.* I wondered, *What was happening?*

Thirty minutes later, I called Jo again and through her tears she told me that Lucy had been put to sleep. Jo explained that quite unexpectedly the dog's health plummeted. They were unaware that she had cancer. I told Jo about Lucy's "visit" to say good-bye and how she "traveled" from Illinois to find me on the freeway headed toward Oregon. I described Hunyak's reaction, which now seemed to make perfect sense. Hunyak and Lucy were strangers, they had never met. Lucy taught me another lesson. Animals, like people, time travel to say good-bye.

Many clients have asked me whether or not other animals in a family feel the loss of the departed animal. The answer is an emphatic *yes!* Following a consultation, this most remarkable story was shared with me. A couple owned Kendra, a twenty-three year old horse. Recently they moved to the ranch of their dreams in Kentucky, and shortly thereafter Kendra died. Both husband and wife believed Kendra waited to die until they had a place of their own. To honor Kendra they decided to bury the horse on the ranch. They had to use a tractor to dig a large grave and in preparation, the other five horses were moved up to the barn.

After Kendra was buried, the other horses were kept in another pasture while the fresh earth settled. When the couple felt that enough time had elapsed and the burial site firm, the horses were permitted to return. The gates were opened and the horses immediately walked over to the burial site, each animal stopping in a corner. The animals stood silently and looked toward the center of the grave site in unison, as if saying good-bye to Kendra. In the days that followed, the horses would not walk on her grave. Months later, the animals continued to circle around Kendra's resting place, showing respect.

Without a doubt, animals know when other companion animals in the family die. Animals feel and they grieve. I can see it in their eyes and I can feel it in their energy. Oftentimes their behavior will change and they become listless and will not eat. They may seem depressed and may appear to walk with their head down. Their ritual habits may become disrupted, including their sleeping pattern, sleeping location, and playfulness. Animals may grieve along with the grieving owner, often checking on their owner— trying to offer comfort with physical touches and questioning looks, as if to say, *How can I help you?* A veterinary check up is apt to turn up no physical problems, but the grief is present, albeit silent. Time is a great healer for both humans and animals, and usually things return to normal in time.

Occasionally, an animal does not rebound from grief and I am called. Murphy, a harlequin Great Dane needed my help to heal. He lost Celeste, his fawn Great Dane buddy, to cancer. Both Murphy and his human owner were drained from Celeste's lingering illness. Celeste and Murphy had lived together and Celeste had been his teacher, his nurturer, and his role model. This was a situation where the first dog raised the second dog. Murphy was now withdrawn and depressed. He had no appetite and was losing weight, becoming weaker daily. When I talked with Murphy he told me he was lonely and uncomfortable being the only dog in the home. I recommended flower essences, in particular Star of Bethlehem, and special love that helped Murphy heal from the loss.

Animals clearly grieve for owners when the owner dies, and in some instances, animals have communicated seeing the spirit of the deceased owner. During a barn call, I was approached by a woman who had observed me for quite awhile as I worked with several horses. Peggy introduced herself and told me there was a horse who needed to talk to me.

Bluebell was a twenty-eight-year old blue roan. As we walked to Bluebell's stall, Peggy told me that the horse belonged to her late mother. Bluebell welcomed me and she was quite willing to talk. Immediately, I felt that Bluebell was an old soul, wise beyond her twenty-eight years. The horse relayed images of herself riding in parades and Peggy nodded that indeed Bluebell and her mom had ridden in almost every Rose Parade in their years together. Then came the difficult question. Peggy explained that her mother passed away only a couple weeks earlier and wanted to know if Bluebell was aware of her owner's passing. Before the question was finished the horse sent me a detailed picture of a petite woman, about five foot two inches in height, wearing glasses. I heard the deceased woman's very deep voice. When I told Peggy what the horse had communicated, her eyes widened in amazement. The description was accurate.

Then Bluebell showed me her saddle and described her blanket in detail. That too was correct and as Peggy relaxed, she whispered that there was no way I might have known these specifics. The pictures kept coming and Bluebell visualized her owner in a medical setting, either a hospital or nursing home. I also felt Bluebell's sadness, a melancholy that seemed to have been around for several weeks. The sadness seemed to coincide with what I envisioned to be a visit from the now-deceased woman. Bluebell showed me Peggy's mom, in spirit, entering the stall, greeting her. Then Bluebell lowers her head as the woman, in spirit, stroked the horse's head.

Peggy clarified the information from the horse by explaining that her mother had been in a nursing home for the past three years. The nursing home was twenty miles away from the stable. Approximately one week before her mother passed away, Bluebell began to show signs of depression—losing weight, hanging her head in the stall, and appearing listless. Peggy was unaware that her mom had gone into kidney failure at that time. Peggy also confirmed Bluebell's message about a greeting from her mom. Whenever Peggy's mom had visited Bluebell in the past, the two shared a ritual. Bluebell would put her face down and wait for her owner to rub her forehead.

We closed the consultation by discussing the future. Bluebell told me she wanted Peggy to keep her and ride her gently. Bluebell was adamant about not wanting to be sold. There was even talk of riding in the Rose Parade one more time. Realizing that Bluebell's remaining life span was short, Peggy began to make plans with Bluebell so that she, too, would have memories of this remarkable horse.

Memories enable a pet lover to keep animal companions nearby even after they die. It is never too early to collect *cellular memories*. Cellular memories are the remembrances we keep, which seem to be filled with minute details that we inhale and store. For instance, when I smell Christmas cookies, I can easily envision myself as a little girl back in the kitchen of my childhood home, baking Christmas cookies with my mother. I see and feel myself kneeling on a chair, mixing the batter, smelling the aroma of the batter turning into cookies. I hear the Christmas music in the background, and I smell Mother's perfume. Cellular memories will span an entire lifetime and enrich our lives.

The special cellular memories I have of my animals will be a part of me as long as I exist. I cherish these memories of my animals. They go like this:

For Hunyak, my "Bud," taking him to Madison Square Garden. I can hear the roar of the crowd and the thunderous applause as we run into the ring. I can feel his show lead in my hand.

For Jessie, my Collie, giving me slobbery wet kisses.

For Magic, my shower kitty, sitting with me after I shower, rubbing against my dripping wet hair.

For Thomas, my magical cat, appearing as I walked under an overpass. "Poof" and there he was on that quiet night, with crickets chirping and his soft meow.

For Jane, my tiny kitten, walking down the barn aisle carrying a gift for me in her mouth—a wriggling snake and watching as it slithered away.

For Peter, my Borzoi pup, seeing his forlorn face in a photo and hearing him say, *Bring me home because I'm supposed to be with you!*

Our animals are gifts. We do not control how long we have them, so we must treasure them for the brief time they grace our lives. When our animals leave, I choose to believe that each animal is escorted to this safe place by an animal messenger. They transform into a spirit world where no animal is in pain, where no animal is homeless, where no animal wants for love.

CARL HIBY

Lydia and the llamas

– Chapter Nine –

How to Communicate
with Animals

*There is nothing so captivating as
new knowledge.*

– Peter Mere Latham

Somehow, on some level, an animal most likely touched you
with a lesson or opened you to a heightened sensitivity. It
may have been an animal whom you remember from your
childhood or it might be an animal in your life now. These shared
relationships bring forth a deeper understanding of life. I believe
that humans and animals offer one another greater understanding
every day we share the earth together.

Humans as well as animals come into this world to learn
lessons. Animals teach us and we teach them. We learn from one
another how to nurture, how to love unconditionally, how to relax,
how to trust, and how to find balance in the world. I believe animals
are here because they are accepting, trusting, and giving of their
gifts. I also believe this is God's plan. I also respect that acceptance
or rejection of a lesson is a matter of personal choice. The insights
and stories in this book offer a window to see the untapped
resources that animal companions graciously provide us.

It has been my long-held belief that any human wishing to talk to the animals has the capability to do so, the only stipulation being an open mind. I do not believe that merely a chosen few have this ability and certainly I was not struck by a "bolt of lightning!" As children we communicated nonverbally and I believe that we can reawaken that skill, which lies dormant in most adults. Nearly all of my clients, even those staunch skeptics, have acknowledged that at least once they have "felt" or "heard" information that could have come directly from their animal. But, lacking validation, the "feelings" remain just that.

Trust the Inner Knowing

The most important message I want to impart regarding animal communication is that although people think it is hard, it really is not. It is just that you can't hold it in your hand. I can prove to anyone who is receptive and willing to try, or for that matter even a skeptic, that animal communication can be learned. Each of us has the potential to develop this ability. Basically what we need is a refresher course to take us back to the way we first communicated before we began using verbal language. It is also necessary to have confidence in your inner voice—to trust that inner knowing. In addition, guidance and counsel from experts are a tremendous help. But always remember that your higher self is the clearest channel for hearing an animal's voice.

At the beginning of my career, I never realized or imagined that my role would be this complex—facilitator, translator, receiver, healer, counselor, and validator. I feel blessed to hear pet owners say, "Just talking with you, I feel so much better!" But for me, the ultimate praise is when an animal being interviewed becomes relaxed and peaceful, and is finally able to release and unload issues that perhaps had been held for a long time. This is the joy in my work, the joy I feel when I hear the inner voice—the voice of the animal.

During a spring horse-group weekend in the Pacific Northwest, my last stop was a visit to an Andalusian ranch. The owners,

Antonio and Roberta, greeted me warmly and asked, "How long can you stay and how many horses can you talk to before you leave for the airport?" Figuring one animal per fifteen minutes, I estimated I could communicate with twelve horses at most. With little time to spare I looked around quickly and immediately recognized utopia. The picturesque setting of the ranch was lifted from the page of a fairy tale. Horses dream of such barns and stalls. But it was the feeling of love and respect for their Andalusians that overshadowed the magnificent land. Obviously, Antonio and Roberta loved and lived with their horses as a family.

As I spoke to the first horse, Antonio became animated, his eyes widening. And as I moved through the barn, entering each stall, communicating with the various horses, Antonio continued to react spontaneously, "Yes! Yes! That's what I was getting! I was right!" What seemed exceptional to Antonio seemed quite normal to me. His enthusiasm reminded me that I will forever remain in awe of the process, and my excitement is rekindled each time I watch an owner validated. Antonio believed his "hunches" but until confirmed, he did not truly accept that he was having a two-way conversation with a horse. Because Antonio paid attention to his inner voice—the voice of his horse—he was now reassured that the way in which he dealt with each individual horse was based on true understanding, a *simpatico* relationship. The information Antonio was picking up was accurate, coming neither from wishful thinking nor his imagination. All twelve of the consultations were recorded on video and would reaffirm for Antonio, long after my departure, what he had experienced.

HONESTY

There are two distinct types of people who have pets: pet owners and pet lovers. Pet owners provide food, shelter, and medical attention—the basics of life. A pet owner remains focused on the main utilitarian reason for having gotten the pet in the first place—the dog is meant to guard, the cat will be a mouser, and the horse is for work. On the other hand, pet lovers, like Antonio, go beyond the necessities and are concerned not only if their animal is happy but how to make their animal's life more wonderful. It is the pet lover who longs to communicate with his or her animal.

It is certainly possible for a pet owner to evolve into a pet lover. The process is slow and begins once an animal touches a human's life and heart. This relationship deepens, the human becomes aware of the animal's feelings and slowly ideas filter into the human's conscience. Eventually these feelings become so powerful they cannot be denied. This transformation can be wrought with frustration and anxiety if the human refuses to honor the shift.

A pet lover, Debbie, watched this very shift take place. Debbie had been brought up with animals and her new husband, Mike, had not. Mike liked animals but never felt the powerful connection that Debbie experienced with animal companions. It was difficult for Mike to understand the magnitude of sadness he witnessed when his wife's family mourned the loss of their dog.

Mike and Debbie bought their first house, but it was Molly, their rescued English Springer Spaniel who turned it into a home. Molly became the first animal to touch Mike's life and his heart. The change in Mike's attitude was subtle and took place slowly, over time. The outcome is that Mike has become an animal lover, now acutely aware of Molly's needs and sensitive to her feelings. Mike now has a solid understanding of how a deep and loving relationship can exist between a human and an animal.

I have always firmly believed that my responsibilities to animal clients and their owners include total honesty about what the animal has communicated, delivered with diplomacy, and thoughtful understanding in order for all to benefit.

Constantly, I am aware of the necessity to step aside and make certain that the inner voice I hear is that of the animal—and not my own agenda or that of the owner. It is my desire to accurately honor and interpret the animal's wishes. A wonderful illustration of this is the time a show horse was brought to me by a devoted owner. The horse did not want to be shown and he clearly sent that message to me with pictures and feelings. I could have told the owner that her horse is deliriously happy and collected the consultation fee. But then I would have had a 1,200 pound animal looking at me asking, *What's wrong? You're lying! You are not telling the truth! I am not happy!* My ethics prevent me from giving anything other than the purist form of communication that comes to me from animals. The animals deserve that level of honesty. And as their voice, I want to be sure their "words" will continually ring true. In the case of the show horse, I told the owner the truth. Fortunately, she respected the horse's wishes, and she switched to competitive trail riding.

After a recent horse consultation, the horse's owner looked me directly in the eye and asked, "Would you have told me if my animal was not happy?" Respecting her directness, I explained that part of my job was to make certain that the animal's thoughts and feelings were understood, but without exception the owner is always told both the positive and the negative. There are times I take a deep breath and pray for gentle eloquence, but never, ever, is the truth hidden from the owner. If the owner is open enough to request the information, then I can help. As an animal communicator on behalf of the animals, this is my responsibility above and beyond all else.

The first time an animal communicator conversed with my pets, I felt excited but somewhat unnerved. I hoped my animals were happy and their needs had been met, but what if they said something different? That was a very vulnerable moment for me. Now, every time I meet with a new client for a consultation, I keep in my mind those feelings of vulnerability. The owner wants confirmation, not judgment—assistance, not criticism.

I often reflect on my co-author's experience and how vulnerable Bonnie felt the first time I talked with Kodiak. Months later she expressed that although the outcome was positive, the phenomenon itself was somewhat unsettling. Bonnie explained, "Until it happens to you, until you have that experience, it's impossible to imagine what it's like—when someone starts pulling detailed information out of the air." So, a word of advice: When you become confident enough to talk to a friend's animal, be sure to temper your words with tact. It is painful for a person to hear that a beloved pet is unhappy with the owner.

Some animal owners are concerned that their pet will send information that could be embarrassing. This is unlikely because animals, childlike and innocent, are not hung up on our shapes, sizes, or physical appearance. They see us as personalities and enjoy us most when we are real. In addition, an animal will not share information if she senses the owner is uncomfortable. There are times an animal has told me, *I can't tell you everything because Mom tells me secrets.* If this happens I usually pick up a feeling of discomfort from the animal when asking the most basic questions. Respecting both animal and the owner, I will only delve further with permission from the owner.

There are other times when animals are relieved to unburden their feelings. I talked with a dog who told me that both children in the family were smoking pot. The dog knew the children were doing something wrong and he showed me a mental image of the kids locking the door to the bedroom. The dog felt uncomfortable and I felt his discomfort. I became the dog and smelled pot and "watched" a reenactment of the scene. This animal was not gossiping about the children, just sharing his worries. I felt responsible to turn this information over to the parents.

There are positives and negatives any time a risk is taken, and being open to hearing what an animal says constitutes taking a risk. We must be prepared for favorable as well as unfavorable truths. The overwhelming majority of my clients want to know how to improve their animals' lives and this positive motivation is most often responsible for that first phone call to me. Medical issues are another major reason people call me. Other owners seek a precise solution to improve relationships between animals in the same family. Two cats might be fighting and the owners want to know who is the bully cat?

On the flip side it is possible that the owner might learn something unpleasant. Perhaps Bianca, the most magnificent animal of her breed, never wanted to be a show dog. Maybe Dexter, the only dog in a family, does not want a new puppy in the family. Or maybe a simple equipment change, such as a thicker saddle pad or different shoes, will relieve a complaining horse. Owners also call for advice about when is the right time to put a sick animal to sleep.

A particularly important situation is recognizing a working animal who is truly unhappy about doing a job. Animals have likes and dislikes just as human beings do. Most service dogs, for example, are thrilled with their career. Occasionally, I will meet a service dog who wants a different life. That was the case with Theo, a yellow Labrador Retriever, bred and trained to be the world's best seeing-eye dog. Theo showed me he wanted to be a hunting dog by sending me pictures of the birds he vicariously retrieved—wild birds falling from the sky, shot by hunters. His trainers projected what Theo was to do and Theo became a responsible service dog. I was intuitively aware of Theo's sadness. Theo did not like his job although he did it to the best of his ability. I am convinced that on some level Theo's owner knew that this dog's heart was not in his work.

Beginning the Process

The animal lover, always hungry for knowledge, is most often the student in my animal communication workshops. The class I teach takes a complete day of instruction, a morning lecture followed by afternoon practice. It is not possible to condense the complete six-hour workshop into a chapter, and unfortunately there is no substitute for me leading a student through the course. What will be missing is my ability to personally guide you, steering you through the questions, and the unique answers you will receive. But, I can provide you with a breakdown of the process and the ensuing abridged version is enough to get you started and whet your appetite. It will enable you to strengthen the bond that already exists between you and your animal companion. However, before beginning, I caution you, as I do every student, that this technique is for the good of the animals. Communicating with animals is not a "party game" for entertainment. All living things must be treated with respect and compassion.

One of the most important elements in communicating with animals is learning how to be present and how to listen with your whole self. I am honored to know that animals trust me by sharing glimpses of their worlds and revealing issues that concern them. So, I want to give them my full attention. While remaining sensitive to the owner, I make a concerted effort to remain open to all possibilities, comments, and feelings from the animal in order to learn and ultimately assist in problem solving. Anytime I listen with my whole self I am focusing on one animal—while simultaneously being aware of the animal's physical sensations and emotions. When I push my ego out of the way, quiet my rational mind, and focus intently, I shift and "step into the animal." Then I trust—and have faith that the animal will send me information.

In teaching animal communication, I have created relaxation techniques that help students more easily receive information. However, when I was developing my own communication skills, it was a matter of being quiet and focusing. I remember simply standing beside an animal and concentrating with all my energy. Sometimes I closed my eyes. Then I would ask the questions. *How are you feeling? What do you like to do? Where do you like to go?* And I would wait for an answer.

After some fifteen years as an animal communicator I still take the time to quiet my mind and clear out the concerns of a busy day. I have become an expert at shelving the problems of the day, putting aside chores, and making the animal's communication the one and only important image to float through my mind. Now I accomplish this shift in seconds. It works anytime I trust, focus, keep minutiae out of my mind, and remain uninterrupted. And yes, I am human! I am fallible. If I have had a stressful day or wake up not feeling confident, animal communication is more difficult.

Only through trial and error, and hours and hours of practice have I accomplished a high degree of accuracy. In the beginning there were times I thought the information I was receiving might be from my imagination and not from the animal. Early in my career as an animal communicator I was troubled about being right or wrong. Now, I stay away from telling a student, "You are wrong."

That student might never try again. Instead, I steer the student in the proper direction by redirecting the questions. It is unrealistic for a beginner to expect the same success as mine and that is why I encourage students, once having taken the class, to return to any future class and practice, gratis. For example, Bonnie has attended at least eight classes, each time becoming more confident, more accurate, and ultimately receiving minute details.

Animals send their perspectives. It is up to the human receiving the message to discern what is communicated. Animals send clear messages, but humans may misinterpret them, and this is the reason that practicing students may be inaccurate. If an animal has a blue food bowl—she will show you a blue food bowl—and you will receive a blue bowl—not a red food bowl. Since humans receive what the animal sends, it is crucial to have validation for the information you receive, particularly as a beginner. Of course, there is always the exception, when an animal bends the truth so to speak. There is a strong possibility that in a family with several cats, the feline responsible for eating off the kitchen counter will not admit to being the guilty party when questioned. It may ultimately be another cat that tattles on the guilty animal.

Tools for Communicating

There are five distinctive terms that become the "tools" of a conversation with an animal. I simply call them the five tools or the technique. These guidelines are essential for establishing a conversation with an animal. Understanding that animals think and communicate primarily in these terms will help to grasp the process. The terms are **perspective, time, emotion, positive terms,** and **discipline.** These five concepts became familiar to me when I took Beatrice Lydecker's class, however once I began seriously working with her the tools took on an entirely new meaning.

The process did not come easily to me, which might surprise you. I could spend an entire day with Beatrice, following her around at a horse group, and ask the first animal one basic question, and get nothing. On to the next horse, and perhaps I would receive one fragment of information. So, I could go through the whole day and "get" perhaps, two pieces of information—that's all. The ability was within me, just as it is within you, yet it needed to be developed and indeed it was a process—a slow process.

More precise and intricate questions unfold once you understand the tools. While the answers may come as a flashed picture, an intense emotion, or perhaps a fleeting, isolated word or phrase, the information is equally correct, regardless of the form in which it was received. Some people receive visual pictures, while others acquire the information through feelings and emotions. Many people receive the data through pictures and emotions, simultaneously. Again, there is no right or wrong way to procure the answers. Just be aware that the information may come to you in a variety of ways.

To my knowledge, Beatrice was the first person to actually name the terms and develop the formula used for animal communication. It was she who realized there was a reoccurring pattern in all her conversations with animals, which led her to identify and name them. Until Beatrice created her animal communication class and instructed students in her technique, (which explains the way in which a conversation evolves) I believe information just twirled around, flowing through the mind—as thought flows through a child's mind.

The following five tools are the backbone of a succinct conversation with an animal.

Perspective refers to seeing or feeling things from the animal's line of sight and sense of space. The world looks far different to a small dog than it does to a large dog. A small dog such as a Beagle will send you pictures of table legs, chair legs, people's feet, and the underside of another dog's belly. A Great Dane will show you counter tops, table tops, the back of the Beagle, and a person's face. You can experiment by getting down on the ground to your pet's sightline. You will be surprised by how different things appear from their height. And imagine how much this perspective can vary from a cat to a large dog to a bird.

An early telephone consultation with two Miniature Poodles

still makes me laugh. Both dogs kept sending pictures of their owner, who they envisioned to be a *giant woman*. I finally asked the woman to describe herself. She was close to six feet tall—a giant to two small dogs!

Sometimes a large dog will attempt to squeeze into a small space. It could be that the animal wants the secure feeling that accompanies tight quarters. Most likely, the dog does not see himself as being as large as he actually is. The same holds true for the fluffy cat who sits in a tissue box, overflowing the sides. The cat is secure in these cozy surroundings and does not feel that his fifteen-pound body is too big for the small box.

At a class practice session, Bailey, a Dachshund, was eager to talk. One of my students said Bailey sent pictures of "feet—many, many, animal feet." Bailey, as it turned out, lived on a llama ranch. From this Dachshund's perspective, llama hooves were what she looked at much of the time.

During a consultation, a West Highland White Terrier told me and then showed me "rocks" in the house. When I gave this information to the owner, validation came in a most unusual way. The rocks were actually Desert Tortoises who were permitted to roam free in the house. Whenever the dog came near a turtle, the turtle would pull its head in. The dog thought he lived among rocks!

Eyesight comes under the heading of perspective. A Rottweiler communicated that while on a camping trip he was chased by a big black dog. The picture the Rottweiler sent wasn't clear, so I knew his eyesight was not as sharp as it could have been. I felt his terror as he ran from the black object. Further questions provided the information I needed to establish that the big black dog was really a bear. The owner confirmed that it was a bear.

Brandi is a Toy Poodle. She is funny and friendly but greets every moving object with a flurry of barks. This is because she is slightly nearsighted. When I became Brandi and looked through her eyes, things appeared blurry. Typically she will bark and then wait for an audible reading. Once Brandi determines that the voice belongs to someone she knows, then she will "get in your face" to greet you.

Time pertains to the fact that animals function on a linear timeline. Animals are not aware of the difference between five minutes and five hours. It is likely that you are given the same exuberant greeting whether you return home from a full day at work or reappear after a quick trip to the mail box. In either case, having left and then returned, you have broken the animal's timeline and are therefore entitled to a welcome! Animals do respond and are reassured by certain words such as "soon."

The importance of time can be demonstrated by Donna's story. Donna requested my help with her newly adopted Shetland Sheepdog pup, Millie. We met in person and the heartbreaking facts of Millie's life unfolded. The cast on the pup's front leg was to heal a bone broken by a previous owner. A pink line with no fur circled her muzzle—where once a tied shoelace kept her from barking. Millie's luck changed when she was abandoned and brought to a veterinarian who placed her with Donna. The immediate problem, although understandable, needed a solution— when Donna went out leaving Millie home, the dog panicked and barked until her owner returned. I explained the way in which dogs experience time, and suggested that Donna begin by leaving Millie alone for just a few minutes, telling the dog, "Mom will be back soon." When Donna returned she praised Millie for being a good dog and waiting patiently. The few minutes were extended in small increments. Before long Donna was able to leave for several hours and return to a relatively calm dog who was happy to see her mom. Millie was soothed by the word "soon" and connected "soon" with trust.

A more complex example of how I use time is when I take an animal back into the past and forward to the future. An Australian Shepherd, Chisom, found a safe haven at "Aussie" rescue. I was asked to communicate with Chisom and find out about his past in order to determine what type of home situation would suit him. When I asked Chisom to tell me what his life was like before he was brought to Aussie rescue, he showed me images of him riding in a pickup truck, visiting a construction site with his owner. This felt like a normal occurrence. Chisom showed me how he jumped out of the truck while he waited for his owner. This happened without the owner's knowledge and they became separated. Of course, there was no validation and I had to trust my gut feeling. Trying to finding Chisom's owner had been unsuccessful. The dog wanted a home and seemed ready to move into the future. Chisom clearly wanted to live with another man, but also showed me children and other dogs. These were his requests and I felt confident that Chisom would feel comfortable in such an environment.

Time seems endless to a horse recovering from a leg injury. The average time for layups vary from three to six months, but they can extend up to one year. The most common question from a horse in this situation is, *How long till I can go back to work?* The best answer is "soon." Animals respond to "soon" just the way children do. I can remember many long car rides as a child, asking my mother, "When will we be there?" The answer was always the same. "We'll be there soon."

Animals live moment to moment, one day follows another. The only exception is their biological clock that tells them when to eat. Therefore, animals live on quality time, not quantity time. Use time to your advantage. Ten minutes of your attention in the morning means everything to your animal. Jennifer began getting up ten minutes earlier and spending this special time with her dog Buffy. Ten minutes of individual attention made all the difference in the world to the dog, whose behavior immediately improved. When Jennifer left for work, she verbally said, "I'll be back soon." Her mind automatically sent a mental impression that she would return shortly and walk through the door. Buffy was left with a feeling of peace rather than fear of abandonment.

Animals can worry about time in the sense that they can have separation anxiety. Bleu is a black Pekingese who has separation-anxiety. He is what I call a "twenty-four/seven"—meaning that twenty-four hours a day, seven days a week he is needy. Flower essences such as Honeysuckle and Agrimony have helped him but he still struggles and worries on a daily basis. That is just his personality!

A more unusual separation-anxiety problem surfaced with a

change in the behavior of an otherwise loving family dog who began to bite guests as they left to go home. The dog showed me he did not want the company to leave. This problem was simply solved by explaining to the dog that his "people friends" would return again. Departing guests offered the dog a treat as they exited the door and the problem was resolved.

Emotions are experienced by both animals and people. My beliefs concerning animal emotions parallel those of Jeffrey Moussaieff Masson and Susan McCarthy, authors of *When Elephants Weep*. In their book they devote entire chapters to the emotions animals experience: joy, shame, anger, fear, compassion, and loneliness—the same emotions ordinarily associated with humans. Passionately they state, "Human beings are not always aware of what they are feeling. Like animals, they may not be able to put their feelings into words. This does not mean they have no feelings."

Being empathetic, I am highly sensitive to the emotions that an animal experiences. At times I have been overwhelmed and embarrassed, but I am always moved when I feel an animal's emotions. One powerful experience that I had feeling an animal's emotions was on a television show focusing on divorcing couples and what happens to their pets. I was supposed to be the "voice" of Angel, a German Shepherd whose owners were splitting up. It was my job to determine with whom Angel wanted to live. I was introduced to the dog in the "green room" (which isn't really green) just before television taping commenced. Within seconds of meeting Angel, a wave of pain and sadness washed over me and tears streamed down my face. I could feel the hurt this beautiful animal felt. The dog was pulled in two directions—trying to please both of the people she loved most in the world. During the television show Angel climbed onto her "mom's" lap, looking for reassurance and the security of two arms around her.

Animals can relay messages about their feelings in some unusual ways. One dog sent an emotional message that was a surprise, not only to a student in one of my classes, but to the owner as well. During a workshop practice session, a student heard music when asking a dog to describe her life. The song the dog "sent" was "Totally Devoted to You," from the movie *Grease*. The dog's owner validated this feeling with tears, for the dog was her rock, her companion, and totally devoted to her.

The depth of emotion that an animal feels still astounds me. At a busy horse consultation weekend, John scheduled a consultation for his recent acquisition, Favio, a handsome Peruvian Paso stallion who had already made a heart connection with his new owner. Favio, who was in training for Western Pleasure, was upset because John had not yet ridden him. John acknowledged this, explaining that although he was a proficient rider, he had never owned a stallion before and felt terribly unprepared to ride Favio. (Because stallions are powerful they are not suitable for everyone. They can be temperamental and are easily excited when they see another horse. Generally, stallions are easily distracted and have been known to fight with another horse with no apparent provocation.)

My consultation revealed that Favio was willing to be gelded in order to take away that extra fire and energy, if that's what was necessary for John to feel comfortable. John was astonished that Favio was so emotionally attached to him and that he would sacrifice a part of himself for their relationship. John agreed to work with the trainer rather than have Favio gelded. John also reassured Favio that ultimately they would ride together.

Positive terms are the only phrases to which an animal responds. Across the board, animals disregard negative instructions. Tell an animal what to do instead of what not to do. A perfect example of what doesn't work is to tell a barking dog, "Don't bark." The positive command is to say, "Be quiet." Likewise, a command, "Don't be wild," would be ignored. The positive command, "Be soft," would register. In a multi-dog family, when one dog picks on another, the owner saying, "Don't hurt your brother," falls on deaf ears. The positive command, "Settle down," works wonders.

My animals understand that "no" means, "Stop what you are

doing!" I then follow with a positive command. For example, "No—be quiet!" or, "No—stay on the floor." You may also play truth or consequences with your animal, saying for instance, "If you go on the couch, you will get a time out."

A horse who is put in cross ties is restrained and must stand still. (The cross ties are attached to the horse's halter.) Helen scheduled a consultation with me to find out why, when her Thoroughbred, Angel, was cross tied, the horse would strike her hooves out at anyone passing by, and then kick with her rear legs. It was easy for me to feel Angel's vulnerability when she was cross tied. She was claustrophobic. I took Angel back in time, asking her to explain her reaction to the cross ties and she showed me her former owner leaving her standing cross tied for long periods of time while the woman made social rounds at the barn, chatting with friends. Angel sent me the feeling that her previous owner was rude. Angel was always scared when left alone in this manner. Although Helen confirmed the previous owner's behavior she was unaware that this was the reason Angel was upset when restrained in cross ties. The solution was to talk to Angel in positive terms. Helen explained that being cross tied was the safest place for Angel to be while being saddled or groomed. In return for standing still, Helen promised Angel that she would never be left alone, and would be untethered as quickly as possible.

When my Collies, Sara and Kane, play they tend to be rough. Sara is apt to bite down hard, and although it is play, I make her aware of her strength. When I tell Sara, "Be gentle" or "Be soft" she is aware of how much pressure she is exerting with her jaws. Sara responds to positive words, but has ignored the negative "Stop it," in spite of the decibel level.

Children learn right from wrong, and can be taught what is safe and what is harmful. Animals can also learn boundaries from us. When we put animals into our domestic environment, it becomes our job to set their parameters. Animals spend their entire life thinking in positive terms and take their cue from us as to what is appropriate behavior. Zsa Zsa is a Cockapoo who is allowed on any furniture in her home. However, when the dog visits Grandma, Zsa Zsa is not permitted on Grandma's antique furniture. Zsa Zsa can differentiate between the two sets of rules.

Discipline, the fifth tool, is a bit tricky. Discipline is what I call a "human-made order." Because humans generally want harmony, discipline is included as a tool in formulating the conversation. Animals are happier when there are guidelines, and guidelines provide safety and security.

At no time do I advocate physical discipline. Animals respond to "time out" for short periods. Losing privileges by being separated from the fun for short periods of time (ten to fifteen minutes) is my preferred method of discipline. Although it is not my first choice, I have on rare occasions used a spray bottle of water (aimed at the body) to get a cat's attention.

A client sought help with two Bull Terriers. Both dogs were strong willed and their play had become accelerated. "Be soft" was ineffective. Yelling did not work. The solution was truth or consequences. The dogs were told verbally that if they were not kind to each other there would be a time out. Two crates were readied and placed side by side. The ultimatum was carried out and for ten to fifteen minutes each dog spent a time out in his own crate. The dogs caught on quickly. Now, if they become too rough, the owner need only glare at them, and the dogs rush into their respective crates by themselves.

These five tools are essential ingredients for a successful conversation with an animal. If these tools or ingredients were thought of in terms of a recipe, each one of the individual entities would be contributing to a whole and finished product. A novice cook follows a basic recipe, and with experience, confidence builds. Some tools that initially demand concentration become somewhat automatic, almost intuitive after continued use. When you reach this level of comfort it is not uncommon to become creative and add your own ingredients, which make your technique more individual. This is precisely what occurs when the five tools are habitually used. Practice brings comfort, which enables you to go beyond the basics and ask better, richer, more detailed questions.

As I became more proficient in the technique, I learned that animals have a great depth of personality. This led me to discover that many animals possess a sense of humor. A remarkable horse, Sir Waldo, taught me that an animal can have a dry sense of humor. This horse relayed his impressions about how *he* trained his human owner, Ron. Prior to Ron purchasing Sir Waldo, the horse had been trained in dressage. Ron was inexperienced in dressage, virtually a beginner—at least that was Sir Waldo's impression! Sir Waldo was not only accepting of the mistakes Ron made, but forgiving as well. The horse was capable of compensating for Ron's short comings. Sir Waldo had a tremendous ego, and rightfully so. The horse was highly skilled and had multiple wins at dressage events.

Another example of how creative ingredients develop with practice is when I "taste" ice cream that an animal has tasted. In a workshop setting, I feel quite pleased if a student "receives" ice cream. More advanced students will often pick up on a specific flavor of ice cream. I have taken it one level higher and can discern whether it is a store brand or a gourmet label—and usually hit the actual brand on target!

How to Talk to the Animals

Step One

Find a quiet place with no distractions where you and your animal can be comfortable together. Some people choose to begin this quiet time with meditation. The normal format of my animal communication class is a morning devoted to lecture followed by a lunch break. Each student may bring one animal to the class in order that we have real animals for the afternoon practice session when the techniques learned are actually applied. Students usually return from lunch very excited, since they are eager to communicate with the animals.

The best way for me to bring the group together and get everyone in the same place is to begin the afternoon session with meditation and focusing techniques. Once students are seated, I begin by asking that feet be placed on the ground so that the body is connected to the earth, as a tree grows from the soil. I speak softly and suggest that the earth's energy move through the body, toward the heart and finally the head. This focusing serves to calm excited students and help get everyone on the same energy level. In my workshop I lead my students in a circular breath exercise, inhaling through the nose and exhaling through the mouth. This preparation takes a few minutes. Other than the sound of the students' regulated breathing, my voice is the only sound heard. I conclude by asking that everyone be open to whatever the animal wants to talk about.

Learning to relax helps me to focus on the animal being. When I first started, I was unable to transition to this level of focus and awareness without total silence. Now, through experience and constant use I successfully communicate with animals in convention halls, on television shows, and on live radio as well as over the telephone. In a very brief amount of time, I am able to shift easily into alpha awareness, creative thought—an awake dream state.

Step Two

Begin communicating with the animal by asking out loud an easy question, such as "What do you like to eat?" Visualize the animal looking at an empty bowl. Picturing a clear glass bowl is often helpful. Silently say the words, *What do you like to eat?* Your words will form a picture. In less than a minute, a response will register. For some people it could be a visual picture of food, for others a smell or a taste. Pay attention to your first impression, for it is apt to be a fleeting blur.

The message will be so quick you may dismiss it if you stop to think about it logically. Write it down! Don't worry about being correct. Your first hunch or idea is apt to be right. Some people receive messages visually, while others tend to be more sensitive to sounds, aromas, and feelings.

When I began communicating, food messages were the strongest I received. Many of the messages seemed illogical then, actually many still seem senseless—until they are validated. One of my earliest food messages came from Trucker, a horse I was communicating with at Riverdowns Racetrack in Ohio. I mentally asked, *What do you like to eat?* Immediately, I smelled and tasted Irish cream coffee. Certain this could not be correct, I repeated the question to Trucker. The answer remained the same. The aroma of the flavored coffee wafted through the air— at least to my nostrils! It was true. Trucker's owner shared this treat with him every morning as she dunked her doughnut in the coffee and gave Trucker his bite.

One of my favorite examples was a consultation I had with a cat named Cameo. I began with mentally asking him, *What do you like to eat?* and tasted champagne. I seriously doubted this message, so I tried again. Once more I tasted champagne. Perplexed and a bit embarrassed I told Cameo's owner what the cat had revealed. A slight grin accompanied her explanation, "Every night I pour myself a glass of champagne and give Cameo a couple of licks. Even the vet doesn't know this!"

When you begin to practice with your animal, perhaps pizza will be your first thought. Chances are that your pet, at some time, has tasted pizza. If you have never given pizza to your pet, perhaps someone else has. Check it out! Often roommates, spouses, trainers, or friends are the culprits. If you can find no guilty party, then there is an extremely strong possibility that pizza is a desired food. Just because an animal desires a food does not mean the food should be given. Use common sense. However, it is quite possible for an animal to desire a food it has never tasted. The animal may have smelled it. Possibly another animal talked about it or even sent pictures of the food. Animals talk to each other all the time by sending pictures.

You might want to take the pizza information a bit further. Pizza has tomato, and tomato is rich in vitamin C. The request you are feeling could easily be an instinctual need. Animals in the wild seek what the body needs nutritionally, whether it is an organ meat from a kill or plant matter that provides a substance the body craves. Domestic animals have similar body requirements.

Shannon, one of Beatrice's German Shepherds, sent me

pictures of grapefruits. At the time it seemed irrelevant, almost silly, so I let it go. Then I began smelling and tasting grapefruit whenever I was around Shannon. Finally, I asked Beatrice about this odd and unusual information, which I thought must have come from my imagination. As it turned out, Shannon enjoyed this delicious fruit often. Shannon was sending me accurate information—pictures, smells, and tastes. If I had trusted my gut reaction more and second-guessed less, I might have asked for verification of the grapefruit message months earlier. I encourage my students to share any message, no matter how bizarre it seems.

During one animal communication class we practiced talking to an Iguana. A student hesitantly shared "olives," which she thought was far fetched. But the message was clear—she saw and smelled olives. This message made perfect sense to the Iguana's owner who validated the information. She explained that the grocery bag in the car contained olives. The nosy Iguana had obviously peeked inside the bag!

STEP THREE

If you were successful in getting a response, or even a sense of what the animal may have communicated, continue by asking the animal the following questions. Remember, always honor that first message.

Basic Questions:
1. *What does your yard look like?*
2. *What does your home look like?*
3. *Who are your friends?* Specify if friends are animals or people—and then precisely identify the animal friend. A dog might be a Boxer or a Boston Terrier or a mixed breed. (Animals acknowledge their own kind in the same way that people are aware that they come from similar cultures. This recognition brings a feeling of familiarity and comfort.)

Once again, trust your inner voice and what you receive. During a communication class I had the students ask Celeste, a Pug, what her yard looked like. Sara, the first student to volunteer, was confused because Celeste had sent her a "picture" of what she thought was her very own yard—a beautifully manicured Japanese garden. Upon further investigation we learned that Celeste's yard was almost identical to Sara's yard. Neither the animal nor the human was wrong.

There have been times an animal has answered my questions about her yard by sending me a blank. I have discovered that this is often the case when the animal lives in a condo or an apartment. In these instances, there is no yard—at least from the animal's perspective.

Abbie's dog, Scooby, answered the question about his yard by sending pictures of acres of lush green rolling lawn, dotted with trees. Scooby showed himself running freely through his property. It did seem as though he lived on an estate—but it is all a matter of the animal's perspective. Actually, Scooby lived in an apartment across the street from a park. The park was "his" yard. It was the place he ran and played every day.

An animal looking through a chainlink fence can ignore the mesh and focus on what is beyond the fence. I have spoken to dogs who thought the entire golf course beyond the fence was their yard.

By now you might be asking, "What if nothing happens?" In the beginning it is going to be difficult because your rational mind will be saying it is not normal to talk to an animal and get a response. The first time I took an animal communication class, I got nothing! I felt incredibly inadequate because I believed that on some level I was already communicating with animals. I couldn't figure out what was wrong with me. But as I truly began to trust the process, bits of information started to filter in. This will happen for you also. As you become consciously aware and acknowledge what is happening, the message sent by the animal will be received by you. For me, the cat's question, *Is my kitten dead?* became the breakthrough and that was when I realized the door had been opened. (See Chapter Three for the cat's story.)

If your animal falls asleep while you practice, let the animal sleep. The mind is always awake. It has been proven that a person in a coma or under anesthesia has the capacity to hear and process information. The mind never shuts off. I believe that a sleeping animal can communicate.

If your pet gets restless and proceeds to get up and leave the room, do not restrain him or her. Animals, like small children, have short-attention spans. Give your pet a rest and try again later. The animal will be very aware that something new is happening. The fact that you are on your animal's wavelength may be very unsettling to your pet. Each animal reacts to communication in specifically individual ways.

Bonnie has followed me from horse to horse during ranch calls when I consulted with as many as twenty-five animals. Bonnie commented on the variety of responses she witnessed as horses waited for their turn to communicate. She also observed different behaviors from horses during consultations. Some horses stand still. Others do what I call "tap dance" because they are impatient. Several horses nuzzle me. A few think eating my jacket is the perfect introduction. And lastly, there is the horse that keeps whinnying impatiently awaiting his turn—really saying, *Don't forget me!*

STEP FOUR

After you ask several general questions and get a sense of conversing with the animal, then you will do what is called the "body scan." This is an important element within the conversation, and may prove invaluable. Many of us, knowing something was not right with our animal, have consulted a veterinarian only to be told that everything checked out and was normal. But still a lingering feeling remained—something was not right. It was merely a feeling, nothing that showed up on a lab test. But the gut feeling said, *Follow your instinct.* It is this feeling that I encourage you to pursue, because your animal is attempting to communicate with you. You do not need to have medical knowledge to successfully implement this technique.

Bonnie had an interesting experience that illustrates this point. Months after taking my class, I had her practice by mentally asking a sick dog, *How are you feeling?* Using the techniques I taught her, Bonnie was quiet for a minute—and then gave me a puzzled look. I asked her to tell me what she picked up. Still confused she answered, "A pomegranate. What does that mean? I've never even eaten a pomegranate!" I encouraged her to keep going, to peel another layer off the pomegranate so to speak. Finally, she said, "I see dark red seeds—they are blood cells—rich and strong. The dog is feeling stronger and healthier." Bonnie was correct. The dog had undergone cancer treatment and was in remission and doing well.

Before beginning the body scan, be aware of how you are feeling physically on that particular day. Be mindful of any discomforts, aches, or pains that *you* have so there is no confusion between *your* sensations and what you pick up from the animal. You will begin by asking the animal out loud, "How are you feeling physically?" Whether you ask the question orally or mentally, your mind will automatically create a picture. Words, silent or spoken, also produce instant feelings.

Then start with the animal's head, "How is your head feeling?" Focus your eyes on the body part you are inquiring about. Then proceed, "How is your neck feeling?" Work your way down the animal's body, asking the same question as you move along.

As you scan the animal's body, you will feel within your body what the animal is experiencing. Your hands are her front paws or hooves and your legs are her hind legs. And if the animal has a tail, you will feel it at your end! Some people have found that keeping a written record is extremely beneficial in remembering the animal's responses. I highly recommend using a journal when asking the animal how he feels physically. Your findings could ultimately help your veterinarian.

I want to emphasize again that you do not need to have medical knowledge to attempt a body scan. By some miracle, which I cannot explain, the information sent to the human compensates for the lack of any medical information. For example, during one of the first animal communication workshops I held, the class focused on Beau, a gentle male Collie. Erica, a new student, seemed unsure about the peculiar image she received. Although Erica did not feel confident, she was willing to share the picture she saw—a bright red, heart-shaped box of candy. I encouraged Erica to go further and open the box of candy. Erica did just that and discovered that one piece of chocolate was missing. What did this mean? For me, the picture was clear—a heart with a hole in it. This was precisely the medical condition with which Beau was afflicted.

It is not unusual for students who have no medical background to continually receive detailed information as they communicate with animals. One student saw a volcano erupt—after which she received validation that the dog with whom she communicated had an ulcer. Pupils have developed itchy skin and watery eyes when talking to a dog suffering from allergies. Others have seen blurry pictures when communicating with a nearsighted horse. A cat with a toothache sent the human receiver a real" toothache. A painful right ear in a first-time student was an infected right ear in the dog with whom he was communicating.

Remember, you are "inside" the animal, so your right ear is the animal's right ear, and your left hip is the animal's left hip. When you interpret right and left as though you are inside the animal you are using veterinary terms and this will be helpful when describing specifics to your vet.

But most of all, keep working with what you get instead of wondering about what you are not getting.

Once the "body scan" is complete, *I always end by telling the animal that any physical problem that I might have picked up is to remain with him or her.* This phenomenon can happen when you push your ego out of the way and allow the physical sensations of the animal to filter in. When you communicate with an animal and become his mouthpiece, you actually assimilate the information sent by the animal. There is no benefit, while attempting to help the animal, to take on and keep the animal's ailments. For example, if I have *experienced* Cleo's sore neck, it would be possible for Cleo's sore neck to remain with me—leaving my neck sore.

I observed such an episode while I was a student. During an animal communication practice session the focus was on Jake, a mellow Basset Hound. While we all performed a body scan on Jake, one student, Trina, became violently ill and ran from the classroom, nauseated. When Trina did not return within a short time I went to check on her. Trina was unable to stop throwing up. Trina had unknowingly picked up the aftermath of Jake's chemotherapy.

If, at the completion of the body scan, you have discovered or felt something wrong, you may wish to say a healing prayer or send healing energy. I simply say, "Dear Lord, please bless this animal." I then envision a beam of white light surrounding the animal. This common metaphysical practice for healing and protection is what works for me. Develop your own blessing and visualization that fits your spiritual beliefs.

Lastly, I always thank the animal for talking to me. You might be surprised, but most animals are very eager to talk. You may also notice the animal looking at you in an odd way. This commonly happens when "mental pictures" are going back and forth between the human's mind and the animal's mind. Most often the animal is intrigued that a person is willing to make the effort to communicate on her wavelength.

STEP FIVE

Practice—practice—practice—but not for hours at a time. Communicating with an animal is work. It is normal to be tired after concentrating and being present. Take a break and try again when you are refreshed.

During a fifteen-minute consultation with an animal I am able to cover all questions, including a body scan. Even as a beginner, it is not necessary for you to spend more than five minutes on a healthy animal's body scan or thirty minutes on a body scan for an ill animal. The more you practice the quicker it becomes.

Remember, an animal has a short-attention span. You may find that the animal tunes you out and walks away after fifteen minutes. That is okay. Just as you are tired, the animal is also tired.

You are on your way to deepening the understanding between you and your animals. You have crossed the bridge between just observing your animal's behavior to understanding your animal's true motivation. At the very core of this connection is the fact that every animal is an individual. It is my hope that this gift becomes the link that binds you closer to your animal companion—and that the link becomes stronger each time you communicate.

Questions and Answers
about Animal Communication

Q: *Can you communicate with every animal?*

A: Most animals have something to say; however, size may play an important role. For instance, a fly will be at a more functional level than a domestic animal. What I mean by that is eating, sleeping, and procreating are the only functions of concern to that living being. It is also important to note that just because communication is possible, the animal may or may not be willing to cooperate. Free will is also God-given to the animals.

Q: *In general is one species smarter than another? Are dogs smarter than cats?*

A: In every realm of the animal kingdom, no matter what group, each animal is an individual---and that individual can indeed have a greater or lesser degree of intelligence. As humans, we need to judge an animal's intelligence by how the animal relates to his environment and individual situations—not by how the animal imitates us! We must be careful not to compare animal intelligence with human intelligence. There are many forms of intelligence in the world and they are all valid and important.

Q: *How do you respond to skeptics?*

A: I actually welcome skeptics, having been a doubter myself. I encourage people to be skeptical of everything—not to walk about unaware—but rather investigate and discover. And most of all listen to that inner voice. Skeptics ultimately become my best publicity because once I have proven to them that communication is possible, they tell everybody!

Q: *How is talking to a domestic animal different from talking to a wild animal?*

A: Domestic animals have many experiences that come from day-to-day life with humans. Wild animals are concerned with the basic needs of food, shelter, and raising their young in the wild, which can be dangerous far beyond the experiences of domestic animals.

Q: *Do animals know whether or not they are an endangered species?*

A: Some of the animals on display at zoos or aquariums are aware. For the most part even if the animals are aware it is not an important issue to them.

Q: How do animals feel about being captive in zoos and marine parks?

A: This is a complex question with an equally complicated response. The answer depends solely on the facility and whether the animal has been "captive-raised" or caught in the wild. Captive-raised animals only know what they have personally experienced but do have instinctual "longings" for their native homes. Captured animals fall into two categories. Some feel "rescued" because their situation was so bad (not enough food) while some are confused and angry, having been taken away from their natural home. There is still another very special group whom I refer to as animal ambassadors. These animal representatives entertain us, help to educate us, and teach us to care for them.

Q: You have said that animals see in color and I have heard that scientists believe animals can see only in black and white. Will you explain this?

A: This topic holds great interest for me especially since my education as an animal-health technician was science based, and scientists question whether animals can see in color. However, ever since I began talking to the animals, they have visualized numerous objects that clearly were in primary colors. Now, I easily perceive secondary colors and hot neon colors as well. Animals have difficulty discerning the difference between certain dark shades as well as some light shades since they tend to look similar. For instance, if a dog is being chased by a dark animal, the dog would show me a dark figure who might actually be dark gray, mahogany, or black. In the same situation, if a light-colored animal was doing the chasing, it could be interpreted as light gray, buff, or white. This color confusion also applies two-fold when I am working with a lost animal who shows me a white house. The house may actually be white, but it could easily be thought of as cream colored or any light pastel as well.

Q: Sometimes I think I know what my animal is telling me. Can anyone be psychic?

A: In my opinion everyone has this ability, which I attribute to God and believe we had as children. I have been blessed to have been guided by a master teacher and I in turn teach the technique to others. Practice is crucial. Keep trusting your inner voice, intuition or gut feeling—whatever you choose to call it. Children are already open to this way of communicating, so please encourage them.

Q: How can you tell what an animal likes to eat?

A: I visualize an empty food bowl and ask the question in my mind, *What do you like to eat?* Less than a minute later I will really taste a certain food. It might be ice cream, pizza, cheese, or vegetables. More often than not, it is everything except what the animal is supposed to eat. Remember, practice is crucial.

Q: Have you spoken to animals who have died?

A: Normally, I decline simply because once the animal's spirit has been released from the physical body, all that remains is love. Occasionally, if the loss is recent and the cause of death unknown, I will make an exception—helping to provide closure and comfort.

Q: Do animals know if they have been reincarnated?

A: Never has an animal told me that in another lifetime she was some other species. However, I have met animals I consider "old souls." I feel that such an animal has a greater understanding about life and is somehow wiser beyond her chronological years. This is the animal who, as she lives her life, seems to do more than just the "job" she was destined to do. These animals are our healers and our nurturers. Every so often I see an extremely deep relationship between a human and an animal—and invariably the animal I find as part of this connection is an old soul. In my opinion, an old soul seems to have been sent to help people with spiritual growth and lend support while learning lessons of their own.

Q: Are some animals more talkative than others?

A: Yes! Some animals are just shy. Others are truly uncomfortable talking to a stranger since the relationship they have with their owner is intensely powerful. Anxious animals may worry about how the information they offer might affect their owner. On the flip side there are animals who are such characters and have such self-esteem that it is difficult to stop them from talking! And lastly, there is the sad situation of the animals who have been mishandled or abused. Although time consuming, I am often able to help these sorrowful animals open up and process through their traumas in order to feel better.

Q: Do you work on more cases of lost cats or dogs?

A: In numbers, cats are ahead of dogs. This is because more people allow cats to go out of the house unattended. In addition, cats are naturally more curious.

Q: Is it more difficult to track a cat or a dog?

A: The smaller the animal the more difficult. It is like looking for a needle in a haystack. Cats are capable of hiding high or low whereas dogs are more limited in the places they can seek refuge.

Q: When I finally found my lost pet, he would not come to me. Why?

A: Once an animal has made the internal shift from being domestic to becoming feral, he deals exclusively with food, shelter, and security for survival. The animal won't come because he is protecting himself. The natural instinct of a feral animal is to stay quiet and hide. With some animals, the shift to being feral can take place within two days, while with others it might not occur for four or five days.

Q: What is it like to talk to birds?

A: Communicating with birds is almost like conversing with humans, because their thought process is closely aligned to ours. Additionally, most bird owners I have worked with devote tremendous amounts of time and energy to their birds and in so doing, establish deep relation-ships. My communication with a bird may almost seem like "baby talk" but the conversation flows. Life spans of between thirty and forty years are average for birds like parrots, while seventy years is not uncommon for Cockatoos. This long life span allows for a vast collection of wonder-ful stories and is the reason many owners make provisions for the bird in a will.

Q: Do young or baby animals have much to say?

A: Breeders frequently ask me to evaluate a litter of dogs or cats and run a temperament check as an aid in assisting them match prospective buyers with suitable animals. The young animal is prone to chatter and feels fresh and new, beginning life with a clean slate.

Q: How do I raise my animal's self-esteem?

A: A positive attitude is easily acquired by affirming and praising the animal on its abilities every day, just as you would do for a child or a good friend.

Q: Do all pets want another animal for a buddy or are some animals content being home alone?

A: Whether the species is a cat, dog, or horse, the preference split is almost fifty-fifty. Some pets are quite happy being alone—*All the more attention for me!*

Q: Do veterinarians believe in your ability to communicate with animals?

A: I feel blessed to have many vets who either refer clients to me or call me themselves. They are comfortable knowing that my job is only to get information. We are all detectives and work to put the pieces of the puzzle together for the common good of the animal. My clients are aware of my clinical training and use of herbs and flower essences, but clearly it is the vet who ultimately makes the diagnosis and prescribes treatment.

Q: How can you determine the cause of a behavioral problem?

A: Many factors enter into determining the cause of such a problem. First, I investigate the animal's motivation. Next, I sense their awareness of the environment, by this I mean chemical influences (household products), nutritional sustenance, and emotional balance. It is on the basis of these elements that I make my suggestions to the owner on how to proceed.

Q: When you talk to animals, are you reading their body language?

A: Half of my practice involves talking to owners about their pets over the telephone. Since these consultations involve calls across the country and around the world the animal's body language is irrelevant and also impossible to observe. Besides, body language is not always accurate. Many mares tell me they do not want to become pregnant, but during their "season" their hormones force them to act otherwise. Some clever animals use body language just to bluff us!

Q: *I have heard that animals are jealous of infants. How do parents introduce a pet to the baby?*

A: Without a doubt, some animals are more sensitive than others and do indeed feel pushed aside when a baby joins the family. Preparation is essential and should begin before the birth of the baby. Once the nursery is set up, a pet should be allowed into the room and told that a baby is coming to join the family. Play a tape with the sounds of a baby crying. The more the pet is included in all the preliminary procedures the better the chances that the animal will accept this new little being as another person who will love them, too. Several clients have shared with me stories of how the family dog or cat woke them up to check on a choking infant who otherwise might have suffocated. (See Chapter Four for one of those amazing stories.)

Q: *What is the best way, in your opinion, to discipline an animal?*

A: Each situation is unique, of course. However, all animals live for our attention and often the punishment that is most effective is to ignore the animal. My recommendation is to put the animal in a "time out" situation, in a crate perhaps. (See Chapter Four for more information.) Then explain why you did this, and what the consequence will be if they don't change their behavior. Yelling at the animal and allowing the animal freedom is not a solution. I strongly believe that you do not need to catch the animal in the act of inappropriate behavior in order to correct her. Animals are quite capable of remembering back to childhood, so they definitely can recall a recent misbehavior. In such a situation take the animal back to the scene of the crime and tell her why you are angry, and why she is getting a time out. "Because you chewed on the sofa you will get a time out for ten minutes."

Q: *Do horses really want to be ridden?*

A: Horses are extremely social animals. Only a small percentage of these animals want little to do with people. Most horses look forward to having their owner "aboard."

Q: Do you believe that dolphins can heal children?

A: The connection between the healing power of dolphins and children has been documented through medical programs available to autistic children as well as disabled children. Sonar vibrations release endorphins in the brain that have a Valium-like effect. Connections between autistic children and dolphins are discussed in Pat St. John's book, *Beyond Words*. Many adults have had similar healing experiences.

Q: Have you ever used your abilities on people?

A: Very few. When I was in training, I did participate in communicating with several autistic children and a coma victim. My expertise is better with animals than humans, and I believe that your own thoughts are your own business. I have used my psychic abilities with people close to me, but only with their permission.

Q: Do you ever work with dogs for the handicapped?

A: Yes, I have worked with Seeing Eye Dogs and with Canine Companions for Independence (CCI). Those are the dogs you might see walking along side or pulling a wheelchair. When service dogs are working they wear some type of colorful backpack to alert people that they are a working animal. These animals are "on duty" when wearing this attire and they should not be distracted or petted. They are permitted access to places such as stores and restaurants where other dogs are not allowed in order that they help and protect their owner. Most owners are concerned that their working partners are happy and healthy. These animals are cherished and treated with tremendous love and respect. Any help I give to the owner is gratis and that will always remain my policy.

Q: Why is it that I often notice my pet staring at me, even when I am doing nothing out of the ordinary?

A: Just the way we humans can pick up "pictures" from our animals, the process reverses itself and our pets are able to pick up pictures not only from other animals but from us as well. So when your pets are staring at you, all that they are doing is watching all of your pictures going by. That is, the pictures in your mind. If you would like to test this theory just "think" about giving your cat a bath and most likely the cat will take off in a blur. Another great test is "think" about going to the refrigerator and then slowly get up as though you are going to head for the kitchen. Chances are your pet will have read your pictures and met you at the fridge.

Q: Is it painful for an animal to be euthanized?

A: No. Long ago the procedure was difficult because the drugs available were very irritating. The drugs used today are not only quick but extremely gentle. As an animal technician I held many animals as they were put to sleep, and I felt their deep sense of peacefulness.

Q: My beloved animal companion is getting on in age and one day I am going to be faced with her death. Do you suggest leaving her body with the vet, cremation, or pet cemetery burial? How do I make such a choice and what would my dog want?

A: Following my premise that an animal considers her body a "spacesuit" the choice of how to treat the body has never been an issue to the animal. The loving pet is accepting of whatever the owner feels is necessary. There is no right or wrong. Once the animal is released from her physical body, the animal does not need to have anything done with it. That is not what is important to the animal. For those who decide to cremate the body, the ashes can be returned in a sealed box or urn. Some people keep the box intact while others choose to sprinkle the ashes in the animal's favorite place and other bury the ashes. I have known other people to place the urn beneath a portrait of the animal. Other possibilities include pet cemetery burial. If you reside in a rural area it may be permissible to bury the animal on your property. Most often, grieving owners who have needed to put the animal to sleep, leave the animal's body at the veterinarian's office. Most honorable vets work with reputable disposal services. To be sure, ask your vet what the disposal service will do with the body. Numerous clients have been comforted by having their animal's ashes returned. Each situation is unique. Whatever you need to do in order to honor the animal is the correct decision.

Q: What are flower essences?

A: Flower essences are a natural way of establishing balance or harmony through the personality by means of wild flowers. They were first discovered by Edward Bach who was a British medical doctor as well as a bacteriologist. For instance, *Star of Bethlehem* aids in grief, trauma, or loss and I often suggest it to a grieving owner—or to a pet who has lost his buddy. *Rescue Remedy* is composed of five essences and is useful for any emergency or stressful situation—for human or animal.

I always carry it with me and I take it before public speaking events! There are flower essences to cover a wide spectrum of emotions.

Q: Are animals forgiving?

A: The answer is an overwhelming yes, with an accompanying explanation. The members of the animal kingdom who live alongside humans can discern the difference between negligence and ignorance. A horse whose ribs are visible to the naked eye would appear to be starving. In actuality, it is possible the caretaker is providing what is thought to be an adequate diet. An unenlightened person who is genuinely innocent of intentional harm would be forgiven by the animal. If, on the other hand, the caregiver was aware that the animal's well-being was compromised, that horse would realize that her hunger was a direct result from a person who was negligent, selfish, or lazy. The horse would then hold the person accountable for such an atrocity and not pardon such actions.

Q: How many animals do you have?

A: My kennel license allows me to have ten dogs. Over the years I have had Collies and Borzois. I also have three goats, one horse, and several cats. Animals value quality time, not quantity time. It does take some juggling but I manage to give each animal some "just for you" time daily. I also rotate, giving different animals a chance to ride with me in the van or sit with me on phone consultation days.

Q: What is the most often asked question?

A: Without a doubt the most popular question asked is whether the animal is happy and if there is anything they can do to make their pet even more content.

Suggested Reading

BACH, EDWARD. *The Bach Flower Remedies*. Keats Publishing. 1979.

BLAKE, HENRY. *Talking With Horses*. Trafalgar Square Pub. 1995.

BOONE, J. ALLEN. *Adventures in Kinship With All Life*. Tree of Life Publications. 1990.

BOONE, J. ALLEN. *Kinship With All Life*. HarperCollins. 1976.

COCHRANE, AMANDA. *Dolphins and Their Power to Heal*. Healing Arts Press. 1992.

HERRIOT, JAMES. *All Creatures Great and Small*. St. Martins Press. 1972.

HERRIOT, JAMES. *All Things Bright and Beautiful*. St. Martins Press. 1976.

KAMINSKI, PATRICIA. *Flower Essence Repertory*. The Flower Essence Society Earth Spirit Inc. 1994.

KOWALSKI, GARY. *Souls of the Animals*. Stillpoint Publishing. 1991.

LYDECKER, BEATRICE. *What the Animals Tell Me*. Harper & Row. 1977.

LYDECKER, BEATRICE. *Stories the Animals Tell Me*. Harper & Row. 1978.

MARTIN, ANN M. *Food Pets Die For: Shocking Facts About Pet Food*. NewSage Press. 1997.

MARTIN, ANN M. *Protect Your Pet: More Shocking Facts*. NewSage Press. 2001.

MCELROY, SUSAN. *Animals as Teachers and Healers*. Ballantine. 1997.

MCELROY, SUSAN. *Animals as Guides for the Soul*. Ballantine. 1998.

PITCAIRIN, RICHARD. *Natural Health for Dogs and Cats*. Rodale Press. 1995.

REYNOLDS, RITA. *Blessing the Bridge: What Animals Teach Us About Death, Dying, and Beyond*. NewSage Press. 2001.

SCHOEN, ALLEN. *Love, Miracles, and Animal Healing*. Simon & Schuster. 1995.

SNADER, MEREDITH. *Healing Your Horse*. Howell Books. 1993.

STEFANATOS, JOAN. *Animals and Man: A State of Blessedness*. Light & Love Pub. 1992.

STEIGER, BRAD. *Strange Powers of Pets*. Berkley Books. 1992.

STEIN, DIANE. *Natural Healing for Dogs And Cats*. Crossing Press. 1993.

STEIN, DIANE. *Natural Remedy Book for Dogs and Cats*. Crossing Press. 1994.

TELLINGTON-JONES, LINDA. *The Tellington Touch*. Penguin Group. 1995.

YARNELL, CELESTE. *Cat Care Naturally*. Charles E. Tuttle. 1995.

ZACHARIAS, MARINA. *"Natural Rearing Newsletter."* PO Box 1436, Jacksonville, OR 97530. (For all animal lovers interested in information on holistic animal health care.)

Afterword

During the creation of this book, Bonnie and I spent many hours together talking, brainstorming, and soul searching. One of the questions Bonnie posed to me was, "What would you most like to be remembered for?" At first, I chuckled, but the answer was clear. "I want to be remembered for my message to the world: *Communication with animals is possible, as long as humans are receptive to the idea and are willing to try.*"

We are born with the ability to talk with animals. Now, we have to reconnect with this inner knowing, and trust it. No longer can humans disregard that the animals can communicate. Their plea, *Pay attention,* must be heard!

With the completion of this book comes the possibility of a new beginning for you and your animals. If you believe in the process, you will experience the magic. And the teachings from the animals will unfold.

For years I have held a vision of what it could be like between animals and humans. In my dreamlike fantasy, I am walking among all kinds of animals who are filled with a gentle peacefulness because they feel understood by the humans around them. Now, as I sit with this image, the possibility of such a world grows even stronger. It is my deepest hope that *Conversations with Animals* will expand this vision of greater understanding and love between animals and humans.

Having shared my story, and the techniques I use to talk to the animals, it is my hope that you in turn will practice and develop this skill. And when you feel prepared, pass it on. As the ripples of communication spread to hundreds, thousands, and millions of humans and animals, we will learn greater love and compassion. I believe the animals are the ones who can gently and patiently teach us these lessons. And in turn, perhaps humans will learn to be kinder and more tolerant of one another.

Animals are a gift, and regardless of how long they live, we have them only for a short time. Treasure the animals and cherish each moment.

Lydia Hiby

CARL HIBY

Lydia Hiby, 10 years old, with her first dog, Ginger.

Lydia Hiby has worked as an animal communicator for more than twenty years. She has communicated with thousands of animals, and their owners, seeking a higher level of understanding in their relationships. Hiby graduated from the Agriculture College in Delhi, New York with an Animal Science Degree, and has worked with several animal clinics as a veterinarian's assistant. She has an international following for her work as an animal communicator, and has received extensive media attention because of her accuracy and success in talking with animals from many different species. Hiby has been featured on "48 Hours," "Late Night with David Letterman," "Jay Leno," "The View," and numerous other television and radio shows. Newspaper features include "The Washington Post," "The Los Angeles Times," "The Chicago Tribune," and "USA Today."

Hiby lives in Southern California with her animal family. She gives lectures, seminars, and in-person meetings with large groups of animals and owners as well as individual phone consultations. For more information, Hiby can be reached at (818) 365-4647. You may also write to: Lydia Hiby, PO Box 282, Sunland, CA 91040. Web site: www.lydiahiby.com.

SHIRLEY FLUG

Bonnie Weintraub, 5 years old, with her first dog, Boots. She called him "my brother."

Bonnie S. Weintraub, raised and educated on the East Coast, comes from a scientific/medical family background. She graduated with a degree in pre-school education and worked with elementary school children for several years, including special needs students. She and her husband have lived in California since the mid-1980s,and have two grown children.

Since Kodiak's death in 1999, Bonnie has been involved in the field of grief counseling for the bereaved pet owner. She is the co-facilitator of a pet loss support group in Los Angeles. For more information contact: Bonnie Weintraub,11333 Moorpark Street #48, Studio City, CA 91602.

OTHER TITLES BY NEWSAGE PRESS

NewSage Press has published many titles related to animals and the animal-human bond. We hope these books will inspire humanity towards a more compassionate and respectful treatment of all living beings.

Blessing the Bridge:
  What Animals Teach Us About Death, Dying, and Beyond
  by Rita M. Reynolds

Three Cats, Two Dogs, One Journey Through Multiple Pet Loss
  by David Congalton
  AWARD WINNER, MERIAL HUMAN-ANIMAL BOND, BEST BOOK

When Your Pet Outlives You: Protecting Animal Companions After You Die
  by David Congalton & Charlotte Alexander
  AWARD WINNER, CWA MUSE MEDALLION 2002

Polar Dream: The First Solo Expedition by a Woman and
  Her Dog to the Magnetic North Pole
  by Helen Thayer, Foreword by Sir Edmund Hillary

Food Pets Die For: Shocking Facts About Pet Food
  by Ann N. Martin

Protect Your Pet: More Shocking Facts
  by Ann N. Martin

Pets at Risk: From Allergies to Cancer, Remedies for an Unsuspected Epidemic
  by Al Plechner, DVM, with Martin Zucker (available Sept. 2003)

Singing to the Sound: Visions of Nature, Animals & Spirit
  by Brenda Peterson

Unforgettable Mutts: Pure of Heart Not of Breed
  by Karen Derrico

The Wolf, the Woman, the Wilderness: A True Story of Returning Home
  by Teresa Tsimmu Martino

Dancer on the Grass: True Stories About Horses and People
  by Teresa Tsimmu Martino

NewSage Press
PO Box 607, Troutdale, OR 97060-0607

Phone Toll Free 877-695-2211, Fax 503-695-5406
Email: info@newsagepress.com, or www.newsagepress.com

Distributed to bookstores by Publishers Group West
800-788-3123, PGW Canada 800-463-3981